Value Flows into SAP ERP® Finance (FI), Controlling (CO), and Profitability Analysis (CO-PA)

Christoph Theis
Stefan Eifler

Thank you for purchasing this book from Espresso Tutorials!

Like a cup of espresso coffee, Espresso Tutorials SAP books are concise and effective. We know that your time is valuable and we deliver information in a succinct and straightforward manner. It only takes our readers a short amount of time to consume SAP concepts. Our books are well recognized in the industry for leveraging tutorial-style instruction and videos to show you step by step how to successfully work with SAP.

Check out our YouTube channel to watch our videos at
https://www.youtube.com/user/EspressoTutorials.

If you are interested in SAP Finance and Controlling, join us at
http://www.fico-forum.com/forum2/
to get your SAP questions answered and contribute to discussions.

Related titles from Espresso Tutorials:

- Martin Munzel: New SAP® Controlling Planning Interface
  http://5011.espresso-tutorials.com
- Stefan Eifler: Quick Guide to SAP® CO-PA (Profitability Analysis)
  http://5018.espresso-tutorials.com
- Paul Ovigele: Reconciling SAP® CO-PA to the General Ledger
  http://5040.espresso-tutorials.com
- Tanya Duncan: Practical Guide to SAP® CO-PC (Product Cost Controlling) *http://5064.espresso-tutorials.com*
- Ashish Sampat: First Steps in SAP® Controlling (CO)
  http://5069.espresso-tutorials.com
- Marjorie Wright: Practical Guide to SAP® Internal Orders (CO-OM)
  http://5139.espresso-tutorials.com
- Ashish Sampat: Expert Tips to Unleash the Full Potential of SAP® Controlling *http://5140.espresso-tutorials.com*
- John Pringle: Practical Guide to SAP® Profit Center Accounting
  http://5144.espresso-tutorials.com/
- Janet Salmon & Claus Wild: First Steps in SAP® S/4HANA Finance
  http://5149.espresso-tutorials.com

Christoph Theis, Stefan Eifler
Value Flows into SAP ERP® Finance (FI), Controlling (CO), and Profitability Analysis (CO-PA)

ISBN:	978-1-5469-7148-1
Editor:	Anja Achilles
Translation:	Tracey Duffy
Cover Design:	Philip Esch, Martin Munzel
Cover Photo:	iStock # 13302363 I bjones27
Interior Design:	Johann-Christian Hanke

Feedback
We greatly appreciate any feedback you may have concerning this book. Please send your feedback via email to: *info@espresso-tutorials.com*.

Table of Contents

Foreword, or: Value flows into the supreme module

If you work in a company that uses the SAP ERP software for its production, logistical, and financial processes, or if you are an external or internal SAP consultant, you will already have thought about how to map your quantity and value flow in the logistical modules of the SAP system and about how this flow is reflected in the accounting modules. How is company business ultimately documented in the Finance (FI) module for external accounting (balance sheet and profit and loss statement [P&L]) and how does it affect internal accounting, especially the Controlling (CO) module, and in particular, gross profit accounting? Following on from that, how can you reconcile external and internal accounting, particularly if you use costing-based *Profitability Analysis (CO-PA)* to map gross profit accounting?

You will find many SAP books that show all the options that the SAP software has to offer.

But don't worry, that is not the intention behind this book! We will not try to explain the basic principles of bookkeeping or cost and activity accounting to you; there are plenty of other good books on accounting that can do that. We also do not intend to describe all the possible tools of the different SAP modules.

The concept of this book is new—there has never been anything like it on the market for SAP books before!

Using a continuous example in an SAP system, we will show you, in an easy and understandable way, the course of a quantity and value flow from its creation in a sales order, through production, up to goods issue and the invoice, and how you can map everything in accounting—from a business perspective and an SAP software perspective.

We will state the required prerequisites in the SAP system in detail and explain how you can reconcile the values created between the individual modules in order to generate reliable reporting.

Reconciliation up to the operating profit is a great challenge, particularly if you use the costing-based form of CO-PA (Profitability Analysis) and values that are not—or at least not immediately—posted to Finance (FI). However, it is precisely this reconciliation between FI and CO-PA that is required in most companies!

Why have we called this foreword "Value flows into the supreme module"? What is the "supreme module"? We will explain this briefly using the following four graphics and with a little smile:

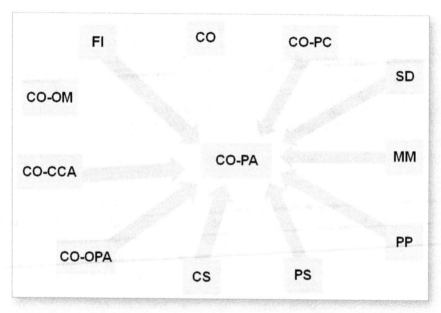

Value flows into CO-PA I

Data is transferred to Profitability Analysis (CO-PA) from many SAP modules.

We will now change this graphic to show CO-PA at the top and all the other modules at the bottom.

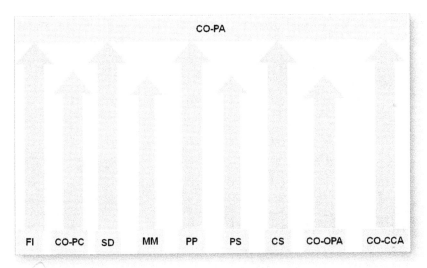

Value flows into CO-PA II

We then merge the arrows.

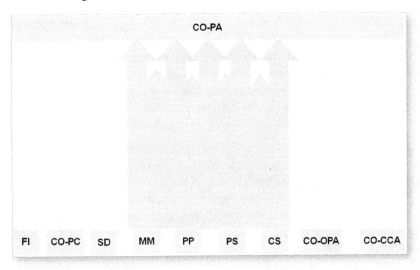

Value flows into CO-PA III

You will recognize straight away that the image looks like a crown. Therefore:

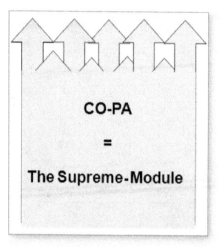

CO-PA reigns "supreme"!

For Stefan Eifler, this book is also a continuation of his work "Quick Guide to SAP CO-PA (Profitability Analysis)" (Espresso Tutorials, 2012). That book describes topics such as the structures and reporting options in CO-PA, characteristic derivations, valuations, and actual and planned value flows in a simple way. The book before you today takes a much more detailed look at the actual value flows into CO-PA but also places great importance on how they can be reconciled in the SAP system, in particular with the FI module.

In Chapter 1 we start by stating some prerequisites so that we are all "speaking the same language" and you can read this book to the end. We briefly describe the organizational structure that is the basis for presenting our value flow, as well as some important master data that we need to describe the processes. We also present a shortened profit and loss statement (P&L) and a gross profit structure; you will also find both of these at the end of each subsequent chapter.

Why, you will be thinking, do they want to literally thrust these structures right under our nose in every chapter? Isn't it enough to see them once? No! At the end of each chapter, we want to show you where the procedure described in the chapter takes effect in the P&L and gross profit structure respectively so that at the end of the book, we can build a bridge between FI and costing-based CO-PA. Chapter by chapter we will take you through the following process steps of a complete logistics sales and production sequence:

- ▶ Sales order (Chapter 2)
- ▶ Production order (Chapter 3)
- ▶ Delivery, including goods issue, to the customer (Chapter 4)
- ▶ Invoice (Chapter 5)
- ▶ CO-PA assessment (Chapter 6)
- ▶ Period-end closing: work in process (WIP) (Chapter 7)

The process starts in the SD (Sales and Distribution) module — the customer is considering submitting a sales order. We will therefore enter a sales order and then produce the product requested by the customer (in the PP module [Production Planning and Control]). After production we will deliver the product to the customer (delivery: SD, goods issue: MM [Materials Management]) and then issue an invoice (SD again).

Finally, we will look at how to map other costs that are not directly part of this process and thus how to post these costs as part of period-end closing.

In the final chapter, we will bring all of the data that has flowed into our P&L and our gross profit structure together and show you not only the course of a quantity and value flow in an SAP system, but also how you can build the bridge between FI and costing-based CO-PA.

In the guest contribution on "The future of CO-PA under SAP S/4HANA", Martin Munzel explains the effects of changing over to the new SAP core product for accounting and why the paradigm change to account-based CO-PA implemented by SAP does not necessarily mean that you will have to sacrifice the costing-based CO-PA that you have grown to love.

Acknowledgments

In writing this book we have received support from many sources and would like to take this opportunity to express our gratitude.

Firstly, our thanks go to our wives Nina and Karin and Stefan's son Jan Lukas; they have all shown a great deal of patience and understanding when, time and again, we were "absent" and busying ourselves with thinking about the next chapter.

Further thanks go to the Managing Director of Espresso Tutorials, Martin Munzel, who has enabled us to publish our combined experience and, with his guest contribution on the future of CO-PA under SAP S/4HANA, has enriched our book.

We would also like to thank Anja Achilles, who proofread the German version of this book, tirelessly familiarizing herself with the new topic and constantly providing us with valuable assistance to make the German version of this practical manual understandable.

For the translation of the original German version into English, our thanks go to Tracey Duffy.

Finally, our thanks go to all the employees at Espresso Tutorials who, with their commitment, have enabled this book to be created.

We have added a few icons to highlight important information. These include:

Tips

Tips highlight information that provides more details about the subject being described and/or additional background information.

Attention

Attention notices highlight information that you should be aware of when you go through the examples in this book on your own.

Finally, a note concerning the copyright: all screenshots printed in this book are the copyright of SAP SE. All rights are reserved by SAP SE. Copyright pertains to all SAP images in this publication. For the sake of simplicity, we do not mention this specifically underneath every screenshot.

1 Our prerequisites for describing the logistical sales and production process

Before describing a logistical sales and production process, we have to specify certain prerequisites from the very beginning in order to avoid repetition and to set down some fixed definitions.

These prerequisites include:

- ▶ *Organizational structure*: How do we map our company in the SAP system?

- ▶ Profit and loss (P&L) structure in Finance (FI): What does our *financial statement schema* look like in the SAP system? (Whereby the focus is on the P&L.)

- ▶ Gross profit structure in CO-PA: Which *value fields* have we defined for mapping our gross profit structure in CO-PA?

- ▶ Materials: How do we define the corresponding *material master data* with the relevant fields for one finished product and two raw materials?

- ▶ *Adjusted standard cost estimate*: How do we create an adjusted standard cost estimate and thus determine the cost of goods manufactured for our finished product?

Because the main focus of our book is on mapping and deriving the value flows of logistical and production processes in Finance, Controlling, and Profitability Analysis, as far as the prerequisites are concerned, we will address only those specific settings that we need. However, we will not show how to define these settings in detail each time—that is beyond the scope of this book.

1.1   Organizational prerequisites

1.1.1   The organizational structures of our SAP system

In our SAP ERP system, the organizational structure is the backbone of the system. All the settings that we define to map processes are based on this structure. Therefore, Figure 1.1 shows the organizational structure that we use to describe the value flow.

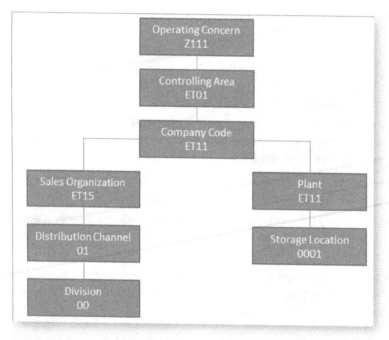

Figure 1.1: Organizational structure

We start our process at the point in time at which a customer places an order for our finished product. For this purpose, we create a sales order in *sales organization* **ET15** with *distribution channel* **01** and *division* **00**. We then manufacture the product in *plant* **ET11**, store it in *storage location* **0001**, deliver it to the customer, and create an invoice.

Because values flow into Finance and Controlling during this logistical process, we have created *company code* **ET11** and assigned it to *controlling area* **ET01**. In order to then be able to transfer values to CO-PA, we have assigned our controlling area to *operating concern* **Z111**.

In doing so, we ensure that we run our process logistically and from a production perspective in order to transfer the corresponding values to **Finance**, **Controlling**, and **Profitability Analysis** (as a submodule of Controlling) in parallel.

Organizational structure

 Make a note of this page: as we go through the book, we will use organizational units from this organizational structure time and again.

1.1.2 Shortened profit and loss statement structure for our value flow

In an SAP system, you create a financial statement structure using a financial statement schema. You define this in Customizing via the following menu path: SPRO • FINANCIAL ACCOUNTING (NEW) • GENERAL LEDGER ACCOUNTING • MASTER DATA • G/L ACCOUNTS • FINANCIAL STATEMENT STRUCTURES.

We will use the *financial statement structure* we created, **ET11.**

For our value flow, we decided on a shortened representation of the profit and loss statement (P&L) to allow better presentation of the analysis in the rest of the book (see Figure 1.2).

Figure 1.2: Shortened P&L structure

As we progress through the process, we will fill this shortened P&L structure with values.

1.1.3   Gross profit structure for our value flow

We will also use a shortened gross profit structure to describe our value flow, as shown in Figure 1.3.

Figure 1.3: Gross profit structure

You define the gross profit structure in the reporting for CO-PA. In the costing-based form of CO-PA, the structure is represented using value fields. Value fields and *characteristics* are the master data maintained in CO-PA. In CO-PA reporting, the lines in the gross profit structure are defined as value fields (i.e., fields that take values) or totals of value fields, with subtotals being created as formulas.

1.1.4 Comparing the profit and loss statement and the gross profit structure

At the end of each chapter that describes posting transactions or procedures required to reconcile FI and CO, you will find an overview that compares the structures described in Sections 1.1.2 and 1.1.3 and highlights the procedures described in the respective chapter.

Figure 1.4 shows the empty overview, while Figure 1.5 shows the same comparison of the profit and loss and gross profit structures but including all accounts and cost elements that we will post to in the course of our process description.

Finance (FI)				Controlling		
		Cost Center	Production Order	Profitability Object (CO-PA)		
P&L	Value	Value	Value	GP Structure	Actual Values	Cost-Based V.
Sales						
Revenues				Revenues		
Discounts				Discounts		
Inventory Changes				Net Sales	0	
Goods Received FERT						
Goods Received FERT						
Goods Issued FERT				CoS		
Production Variance				Production Variance		
Material Costs						
Consumption Raw Mat.				Material Costs		
Material Overhead				Material Overhead		
Manufacturing Costs						
Direct Labor				Direct Labor		
Manufacturing Overhead				Manufact. Overhead		
Wages Production						
Salary Prod. Mgt.				Gross Profit	0	
Wages Purchase						
Others						
Assessment CCA->CO-PA				Assessments		
EBIT	0	0	0	EBIT	0	

Figure 1.4: Comparison of the P&L and gross profit structures

Finance (FI)		Controlling				
		Cost Center	Production Order	Profitability Object (CO-PA)		
P&L	Value	Value	Value	GP Structure	Actual Values	Cost-Based Vals.
Sales						
Revenue				Revenue		
Account 600000				CE 600000 Type 11		
Discounts				Discounts		
Account 600001				CE 600001 Type 12		
Inventory Changes				Net Sales	0	
Goods Received FERT						
Account 711111			CE 711111 Type 1			
Work in Progress						
Account 791111			CE 791111 Type 1			
Goods Issued FERT				CoS		
Account 893015				(VPRS)		
Production Variance				Production Variance		
Account 722222			CE 722222 Type 1	CE 722222 Type 1		
Material Costs						
Consumption Raw Mat.				Material Costs		
Account 733331			CE 733331 Type 1			
Account 733332			CE 733332 Type 1			
Material Overhead		CE 941111 Type 41	CE 941111 Type 41	Material Overhead		
Manufacturing Costs						
Direct Labor		CE 943111 Type 43	CE 943111 Type 43	Direct Labor		
Manufacturing Overhead		CE 941222 Type 41	CE 941222 Type 41	Manufact. Overhead		
Wages Production						
Account 744444		CE 744444 Type 1				
Wages Purchase				Gross Profit	0	
Account 755555		CE 755555 Type 1				
Others				Assessments		
Assessment CCA->CO-PA		CE 942555 Type 42		CE 942555 Type 42		
EBIT	0	0	0	**EBIT**	0	

Figure 1.5: Overview of FI/CO/CO-PA, including accounts

The P&L accounts are usually simultaneously primary cost elements in Controlling; in contrast, secondary cost elements apply exclusively in Controlling.

Figure 1.6 explains the meaning of the accounts/cost elements used in this book.

Finance		Controlling				
Account	Description	Cost Element	Description	Primary/Secondary	Cost Element Category	Description
600000	Revenues	600000	Revenues	primary	11	Revenues
600001	Discounts	600001	Discounts	primary	12	Sales Deduction
711111	Finished Good 1	711111	Finished Good 1	primary	1	Primary Costs/Cost-Reducing Revenues
791111	Inventory in Process	791111	Inventory in Process	primary	1	Primary Costs/Cost-Reducing Revenues
893015	Cost of Goods Sold					
722222	Price Differences	722222	Price Differences	primary	1	Primary Costs/Cost-Reducing Revenues
733331	Consump. Raw Mat.1	733331	Consump. Raw Mat.1	primary	1	Primary Costs/Cost-Reducing Revenues
733332	Consump. Raw Mat.2	733332	Consump. Raw Mat.2	primary	1	Primary Costs/Cost-Reducing Revenues
		941111	Purchasing	secondary	41	Overhead Rates
		943111	Personnel Hours	secondary	43	Internal Activity Allocation
		941222	Production Manager	secondary	41	Overhead Rates
744444	Direct Labor Costs	744444	Direct Labor Costs	primary	1	Primary Costs/Cost-Reducing Revenues
755555	Salaries	755555	Salaries	primary	1	Primary Costs/Cost-Reducing Revenues
		942555	COPA Assessment	secondary	42	Assessment

Figure 1.6: Account/cost element overview

At the start of our comparison of the P&L with the gross profit structure, we assume that initial expense postings have taken place in the period. These P&L accounts were created simultaneously as *cost elements* of type **1** (*primary cost element*), which means that they are also valid for CO. Therefore, they require a *controlling-relevant account assignment*—we have used a cost center in each case for this purpose. The following expense postings form the basis for this account assignment:

▶ **Wages Production** (account 744444) to cost center KS1 in the amount of **EUR 1500**

▶ Production management salaries (**Salary Prod. Mgt.**) (account 755555) to cost center KS4 in the amount of **EUR 1000**

▶ **Wages Purchase** (account 744444) to cost center KS3 in the amount of **EUR 1000**

Figure 1.7 shows the resulting FI/CO/CO-PA overview at the start of our example.

Finance (FI)		Controlling				
		Cost Center	Production Order	Profitability Object (CO-PA)		
P&L	Value	Value	Value	GP Structure	Actual Values	Cost-Based V.
Sales						
Revenues				Revenues		
Discounts				Discounts		
Inventory Changes				Net Sales	0	
Goods Received FERT						
Goods Received FERT						
Goods Issued FERT				CoS		
Production Variance				Production Variance		
Material Costs						
Consumption Raw Mat.				Material Costs		
Material Overhead				Material Overhead		
Manufacturing Costs						
Direct Labor				Direct Labor		
Manufacturing Overhead				Manufact. Overhead		
Wages Production	1500	1500				
Salary Prod. Mgt.	1000	1000		Gross Profit	0	
Wages Purchase	1000	1000				
Others						
Assessment CCA->CO-PA				Assessments		
EBIT	3500	3500	0	EBIT	0	

Figure 1.7: Initial FI/CO/CO-PA overview

Without the logistical sales and production process even having begun, we have already posted expenses in the amount of **EUR 3500**. Let us hope that during the course of our description of the value flow, we post some positive transactions so that we do not have to report a deficit of **EUR 3500** at the end of the period.

1.2   The standard material costing

In order to create a *standard material costing* for the finished product that we want to produce, we have to maintain the *product master data* for the finished product and the components required to produce it correctly.

In an integrated ERP system, the importance of correctly maintained master data should be familiar to everyone because these settings control processes in the system and many different modules access the same information in this master data.

Therefore, in the following section, we will look at the product master data.

1.2.1   Product master data

General definition of product master data

Views of a material are created for each department. The respective departments can then maintain the views according to their own requirements.

For our value flow, we create three materials in the system:

- ▶ Our **sales product** (**FERT1**), which we want to manufacture and sell ourselves
- ▶ Two **raw materials** (**ROH1** and **ROH2**), which we want to use in the manufacture of our product

In the same way as for the P&L structure, for our materials we concentrate on the views and fields that are necessary and interesting for our value flow:

▶ **Material number, material short text, base unit of measure**
The *material number* is the key that defines our product in the SAP system uniquely. The *material short text* is the corresponding description of our product. The *base unit of measure* represents the unit in which the stocks are managed in the SAP system.

▶ **Procurement type**
We use the *procurement type* to define whether the product is produced in our company (**E**) or is purchased from suppliers (**F**). The procurement indicator will be interesting in the next chapter when we discuss the adjusted standard cost estimate for the sales product that we are manufacturing ourselves.

▶ **Valuation class**
The *valuation class* determines the general ledger accounts posted to in a movement of goods, for example. You have to assign the valuation class to the respective general ledger accounts for the corresponding procedures in Customizing (transaction OBYC). In the course of our value flow, we will refer to transaction OBYC repeatedly to explain, for the individual logistical or production procedures, why the corresponding account is used for the respective posting.

▶ **Price control**
The *price control* specifies how the stock of a material is to be valued: either with the standard price (**S**) or with the moving price (**V**).
- The *S price* is a fixed price that does not change for goods movements or when invoices are entered. It should always be set for products manufactured in-house. The S price is determined using material costing, which we will look at more closely in the next section.
- The *V price*, also referred to as the *moving price*, however, can change for every goods receipt movement or invoice entry. It is always the result of the total material value divided by the material stock and should always be set for products procured externally.

▶ **"Standard cost estimate" area**
In the costing view, the *standard cost estimate* area is important for our finished product. We will look at how these standard cost estimate fields are filled in more detail in the next chapter.

Creating the relevant material master data for describing our logistical sales and production process

Three materials are important in the further course of this book:

▶ **FERT1 – Finished product 1**

We have created our only finished product, which we want to sell, in plant **ET11** with material number **FERT1**. The material text is **Finished product 1**. The base unit of measure is **piece (PC)** and the valuation class is **7920**. The price control is set to **S**. Because we want to manufacture this product ourselves, the procurement indicator is **E**.

▶ **RAW MATERIAL 1** and **RAW MATERIAL 2**

We have created our raw materials in plant **ET11** with material numbers **RAW MATERIAL 1** and **RAW MATERIAL 2**. In each case, the base unit of measure is **piece**. The valuation classes are **3000** and **3001** respectively. In each case, the price control is set to **V** (moving price).

We procure these raw materials externally and therefore we have set the procurement indicator to **F**.

We can look at material master data in the SAP system with transaction MM03; we create it with transaction MM01.

1.2.2   Material costing

As already mentioned in the introduction, in this section, we do not explicitly explain how to create a material costing with all the fine details. At this point, it is only important to describe the material costing components for the costing of our finished product **FERT1** that we require as a prerequisite for the value flow we are describing.

The material costing answers the following important question: What does the product we are manufacturing cost?

We create the material costing with transaction CK11N; we use transaction CK13N to display a material costing that has already been created.

For our finished product **FERT1** we have created an initial material costing, resulting in a value of **EUR 1650** (see Figure 1.8).

Figure 1.8: Adjusted standard cost estimate

How do we get to this costing value? We will look at how this value is derived more closely on the next pages.

Cost component RAW MATERIALS

Let's start with the cost component *raw materials*. To obtain this value, we value the quantities of raw materials required to manufacture our finished product at the respective prices defined in the material masters for the raw materials.

The *bill of material* defines which raw materials are used and in what quantity. To manufacture our fictitious finished product, we need one piece of **raw material 1** and two pieces of **raw material 2**.

Accordingly, we have created the bill of material shown in Figure 1.9 for our finished product.

We can display bills of material with transaction CS03; we create them with transaction CS01.

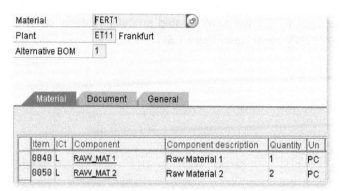

Figure 1.9: Bill of material for FERT1

We purchased **RAW MATERIAL 1** for **EUR 400** per piece and **RAW MATE-RIAL 2** for **EUR 300** per piece (see Figure 1.10 and Figure 1.11).

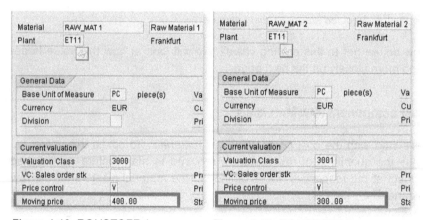

Figure 1.10: ROHSTOFF 1   Figure 1.11: ROHSTOFF 2

Assuming that we did not have any stocks of the respective raw materials on hand, this results in a moving price of **EUR 400** and **EUR 300** respectively, which is defined in the ACCOUNTING 1 view for the respective product master record.

This results in the following calculation for the cost component **Raw Materials**:

(**1 piece** of **RAW MATERIAL 1**, valued at **EUR 400**) +

(**2 pieces** of **RAW MATERIAL 2**, valued at **EUR 300**)

= **EUR 1000 costs for raw materials**.

Cost component MATERIAL OVERHEAD

The next cost component we will look at is the *material overhead*.

These costs are used to charge costs related to the procurement of materials—such as the purchasing costs, to a product. A percentage-based overhead is applied to a base (e.g., raw material costs).

The material overhead rate is calculated by dividing the material overhead (numerator) by the direct material costs (denominator).

The result of the calculation is reported as the material overhead.

In order to be able to determine the material overhead, we have to define a *costing sheet* in Customizing under CONTROLLING • PRODUCT COST CONTROLLING • PRODUCT COST PLANNING • BASIC SETTINGS FOR MATERIAL COSTING • DEFINE COSTING SHEET (see Figure 1.12).

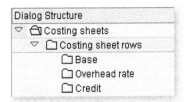

Figure 1.12: Components of the costing sheet

We have named the costing sheet **ZZUSCH**. For the material overhead, we have entered appropriate information for the sheet lines BASE, OVERHEAD RATE, and CREDIT.

Figure 1.13 shows the settings for our costing in detail.

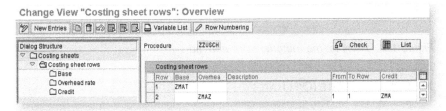

Figure 1.13: Costing sheet for the material overhead

► BASE

We have defined the consumption accounts for our raw materials as base **ZMAT**. These accounts result from the *account determination* (transaction OBYC) via the valuation classes.

In transaction OBYC, we have defined account **733331 Consumption of raw material 1** for consumption of raw materials from valuation class **3000** and account **733332 Consumption of raw material 2** for valuation class **3001** (see Figure 1.14).

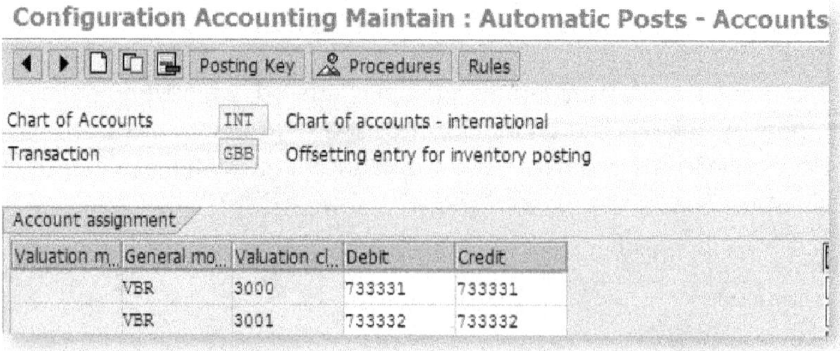

Configuration Accounting Maintain : Automatic Posts - Accounts

◀ ▶ ☐ ☐ ☐ | Posting Key | Procedures | Rules

| Chart of Accounts | INT | Chart of accounts - international |
| Transaction | GBB | Offsetting entry for inventory posting |

Account assignment

Valuation m...	General mo...	Valuation cl...	Debit	Credit	
	VBR	3000	733331	733331	[
	VBR	3001	733332	733332	[

Figure 1.14: MM account determination

These are the accounts that we have defined as the calculation base **ZMAT** for the material overhead rate (see Figure 1.15).

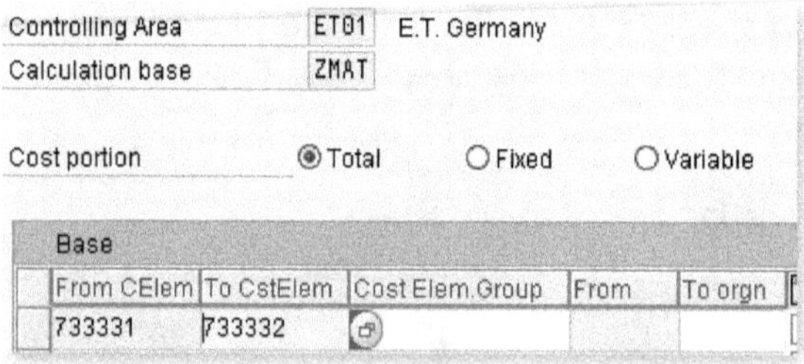

| Controlling Area | ET01 | E.T. Germany |
| Calculation base | ZMAT | |

Cost portion   ⊙ Total   ○ Fixed   ○ Variable

Base

From CElem	To CstElem	Cost Elem.Group	From	To orgn	[
733331	733332	⊡			[

Figure 1.15: Base for the material overhead rate

► OVERHEAD RATE (O/H RATE)

We have set the overhead rate **ZMAZ** to **5.00%** (see Figure 1.16).

| O/H Rate | ZMAZ | | | | | | |
| Dependency | D030 | Overhead Type/Company Code | | | | | |

Overhead rate							
Valid from	To	CO Area	Ovrhd type	CoCo	Percentage		Unit
01/01/2015	12/31/2016	ET01	1	ET11	5.000		%
01/01/2015	12/31/2016	ET01	2	ET11	5.000		%

Figure 1.16: Material overhead rate

Overhead type

 Before you ask why these two lines appear, here is a short explanation: the overhead type is differentiated in **1** for **actual overhead** and **2** for **planned overhead**. Therefore, we could theoretically specify different percentage rates for the actual and planned overheads but this is not planned for our example.

▶ CREDIT

The CREDIT defines the *cost center* to be credited (in our example, the purchasing cost center **KS3**) as well as the cost element with which the credit to the cost center and the debit to our product are to be posted—in our case, cost element **941111** (Material Overhead) (see Figure 1.17).

| Controlling Area | ET01 | E.T. Germany |
| Credit | ZMA | |

Credit					
Valid to	Cost Elem.		OrGp	Fxd %	Cost Center
12/31/2015	941111			*	KS3

Figure 1.17: Material overhead credit

We have thus defined that cost center **KS3** is credited with part of the costs. The finished product **FERT1** is debited with these costs.

Cost element type

 We have created cost element **941111** with *cost element type* **41**. The cost element type defines the procedures in Controlling that the respective cost elements are used for. Cost element type **41** is the procedure for overheads.

This results in the following calculation for the cost component **Material Overhead**:

Base raw materials EUR 1000 * overhead rate 5%

= EUR 50 material overhead

Cost component PRODUCTION LABOR

Let us return to the material costing for our sales product **FERT1** in Figure 1.8 and look at the cost component **Production Labor** in more detail.

These production costs are the result of the hours worked and the *activity price* for a working hour. This is simply the price that we have to pay for a working hour to manufacture our product and it is derived from the activity price planning, while the working hours to be performed result from information in the *routing*.

We use the *work center* to define where our product is manufactured. For our example, we have decided on a purely personnel work center (see Figure 1.18) at which only personnel hours are performed.

We have assigned cost center **KS1** (Production 1) to our work center. Why a cost center? Well, for example, employees work at a work center and they have to be paid at the end of the month. These labor costs are posted to this cost center.

We can look at a work center with transaction CR03; we create a work center with transaction CR01.

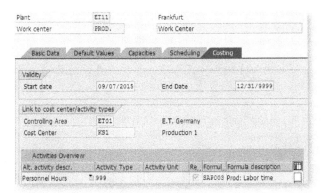

Figure 1.18: Work center for FERT1

In order to be able to charge the costs for our cost center or work center to our product at the end of the day, we have created *activity type* **999** (Personnel Hours) (see Figure 1.19) and assigned it to cost element **943111** (Personnel Hours).

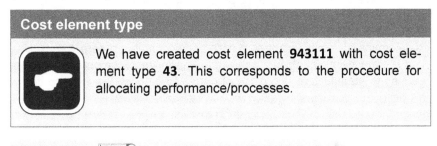

Cost element type

We have created cost element **943111** with cost element type **43**. This corresponds to the procedure for allocating performance/processes.

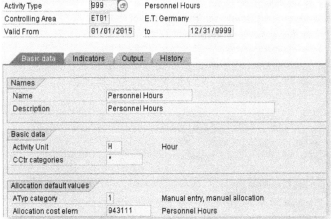

Figure 1.19: Activity type

To define how many personnel hours we need to manufacture our product, we have created a routing for our finished product (see Figure 1.20).

We can look at a routing with transaction CA03; we create a routing with transaction CA01.

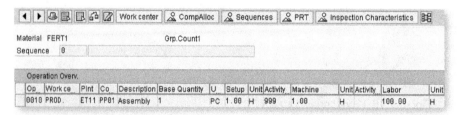

| ◄ | ► | 🖨 | 📋 | 📋 | 🔍 | ✏ | Work center | 👤 CompAlloc | 👤 Sequences | 👤 PRT | 👤 Inspection Characteristics | ⊞ |

Material FERT1   Grp.Count1

Sequence   0

Operation Overv.

	Op	Work ce	Plnt	Co	Description	Base Quantity	U	Setup	Unit	Activity	Machine		Unit	Activity	Labor		Unit
	0010	PROD.	ET11	PP01	Assembly	1		PC	1.00	H	999	1.00		H		100.00		H

Figure 1.20: Routing for FERT1

According to this routing, to manufacture one piece of our sales product, we need **100** labor hours of an employee at the work center **PROD.** When we produce one piece of the finished product, cost center KS1 is debited. But where do the costs come from?

To determine the costs, we need a price per working hour (here, the working hour is the activity type **999**) which is then multiplied by the number of hours required to manufacture one piece of our sales product. We have to define this price, the activity price which we have already discussed, for the combination "cost center and activity type" in the activity price planning, as shown in Figure 1.21.

We perform the activity price planning with transaction KP26. We can display the activity price planning with transaction KP27.

Display Activity Type/Price Planning: Overview Screen

| ✎ | 🔍 | 📋 | 📋 | 📋 | ✏ | 🖩 Line items | 📋 | 📋 |

Version	0		Plan/Act - Version
Period	1	To 12	
Fiscal Year	2017		
Cost Center	KS1		Production 1

Activity	Unit	Variable pri	Alloc. cost element
999	H	5.00	943111

Figure 1.21: Activity price planning

Activity price calculation

The activity price is usually determined as part of the annual budget planning. Here, we define what a cost center should produce in a period, that is, how many personnel hours it outputs to manufacture finished products. To determine the activity price that is used to charge all costs of the cost center to the individual products during a period, we divide the total costs of this cost center by the hours used.

The combination of the information from the work center, routing, and activity price planning produce in total the costs for production personnel:

100 (labor) hours from work center **PROD.** according to the routing * **EUR 5** per labor hour from the activity price planning cost center KS1/activity type **999 = EUR 500** for "Production personnel"

Cost component MANUFACTURING OVERHEAD

Finally, we will now look at the cost component *manufacturing overhead* from our material costing (see Figure 1.8). Just like for the material overhead, we calculate this via a percentage-based overhead defined in the costing sheet.

The manufacturing overhead rate is a result of the quotient manufacturing overhead (numerator) and direct production costs (denominator).

Because we have already described the costing sheet, we will only address the specific settings for the manufacturing overhead briefly (see Figure 1.22).

Figure 1.22: Costing sheet for manufacturing overhead costs

▶ BASE (see Figure 1.23)
We have defined our personnel hours clearing account **943111** (Personnel Hours) as the base.

Figure 1.23: Base for the manufacturing overhead

▶ OVERHEAD RATE (see Figure 1.24)
We have set the overhead rate at **20.00%**.

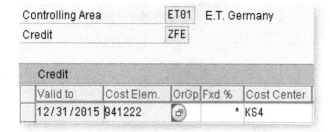

Figure 1.24: Manufacturing overhead rate

▶ CREDIT (see Figure 1.25)
We have defined cost center **KS4** (Production Management) as the credit cost center. We use cost element **941222** (Manufacturing Overhead) as the overhead cost element, again with cost element type **41** for overheads.

Controlling Area	ET01	E.T. Germany
Credit	ZFE	

	Valid to	Cost Elem.	OrGp	Fxd %	Cost Center
	12/31/2015	941222		*	KS4

Figure 1.25: Credit for manufacturing overhead costs

This results in the following manufacturing overhead costs for the costing for our sales product FERT1:

Base "Production personnel" **EUR 500** (determined in the previous section) * overhead rate **20%** = **EUR 100** manufacturing overhead costs

We have now explained all four cost components of our material costing.

When you save this material costing, it receives the status **KA** for "costed". As soon as you hold the costing with transaction CK24, you will see the costed value in the amount of **EUR 1650** in the future planned price. If you go one step further and release the held costing, the current planned price for your product is entered.

Releasing the material costing

 Be careful! When you release the costing you also up-date the standard price (S price) in the view AC-COUNTING 1. This price is used to value the stock that you have of your sales product on hand. You therefore simultaneously revalue the stock of your product and automatically post this stock value to the balance sheet and profit and loss statement.

When you release a material costing, you should always be aware that you are also revaluing the stock of your product. Depending on the volume of stock on hand, this can lead to significant stock change postings if your material costing is different to the previous one.

In our example, however (see Figure 1.26), we have entered the material costing for our finished product **FERT1** in the STANDARD PRICE field for our material (we do not have any stock of the product on hand).

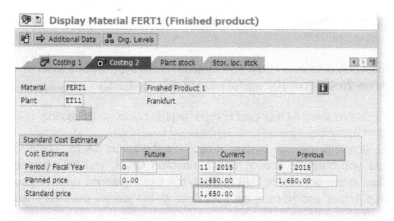

Figure 1.26: Standard price for FERT1

We have thus met all the prerequisites for running our logistical sales and production process. This process consists of the following process steps:

1. Sales order

2. Production order

3. Delivery, incl. goods issue to the customer

4. Invoice

5. CO-PA assessment

6. Work in process (WIP)

We will explain these six process steps in the next chapters.

2 The sales order

Let's assume that our competitive product is known on the market and is enjoying a certain level of demand. Where does the business sequence begin in a logistical sales and production process? Correct: based on an inquiry, an offer, and potentially sales negotiations, the customer places a *sales order* which we want to enter and process in our SAP ERP system.

What happens in this process in an integrated system? The sales order is initially processed in the SAP module Sales and Distribution (SD). The main objective here is to create a sales order in the SAP system, to print it out where applicable, and to send an order confirmation to the customer. Other interesting things also take place which are relevant for accounting: on the one hand there is a *price calculation* for the product to be sold, and when we save the sales order, line items are written to Profitability Analysis (CO-PA) and we can use these line items for *sales order controlling*. **However, the sales order does not yet trigger any postings in the balance sheet or profit and loss statement!** Nevertheless, it does set the course for the subsequent posting of the invoice in Finance (FI) and Controlling (CO).

Therefore, in this chapter, we want to address the following important points:

► How does the SAP system find the prices and conditions relevant for the sales order and how does it use these to calculate the price?

► In terms of time, how far apart are the sales order and the subsequent invoicing? The answer to this question influences whether we transfer sales order data to CO-PA now or when we issue the invoice.

► Do we want to collect revenues and costs on our sales orders to then settle them to CO-PA later, for example, or do we transfer the revenues, discounts, and rebates as well as the costing-based material and production costs to CO-PA directly?

The interface of the SD module is the most important for transferring data to CO-PA. This is not surprising because CO-PA was designed as a sales controlling tool for transferring sales order data and then later the corresponding invoice data to CO-PA.

However, not every company transfers sales order data to CO-PA; many transfer only invoice data from SD to CO-PA. For companies where there is a long period of time between receipt of the sales order and invoicing, the recommendation is to also transfer the sales order data. There are two arguments in favor of this: on the one hand, the incoming order already shows how the business situation of your company will develop. On the other hand, you can use the sales order data to build up *orders on hand reporting* in CO-PA. When you have subsequently also transferred the invoice data, by subtracting the sales order data and invoice data, you can report the orders on hand in reporting for CO-PA—and for all characteristics that you also transfer to CO-PA with the sales order or the invoice.

If you configure the Customizing for your sales orders such that the orders are not collectors for revenues and costs, you can even subsequently transfer your invoice data to CO-PA in real time. If this were not the case, the invoice would first return the data to the sales order and you would then have to settle this order to CO-PA. Depending on how often you undertake such settlement, this can potentially delay important findings in sales controlling because the required information is provided too late.

2.1   Creating a sales order

We will now create a sales order in the SD module of the SAP system using transaction VA01. To do this, enter a *sales document type* and a *sales area* and confirm your entries. In SD, a sales area always consists of three organizational characteristics: the sales organization, distribution channel, and division. In our example system, we use sales document type (ORDER TYPE field) **TA** and sales organization **ET15**, distribution channel **01**, and division **00** (see Figure 2.1).

For our customer **K1**, we enter an order in which the customer has ordered one piece of our sales product **FERT1**. Figure 2.2 shows an overview with the relevant details.

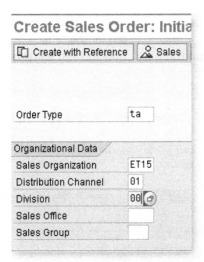

Figure 2.1: Initial screen for creating a sales order

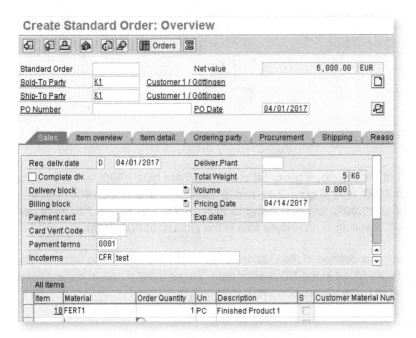

Figure 2.2: Overview of the creation of a sales order

In the top right-hand corner you can see the net value of **EUR 6000**. Where did the system get this value from? On the CONDITIONS tab for the order item (see Figure 2.3) we can find further information about how this net value is calculated.

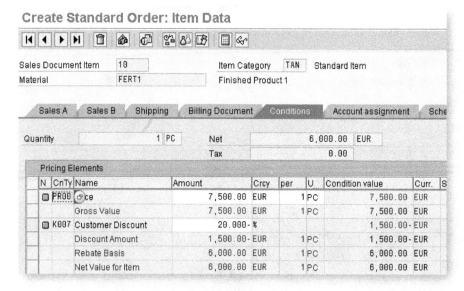

Figure 2.3: Conditions of the sales order item

2.2 SD pricing

As part of the pricing, a gross list price (condition type **PR00**) in the amount of **EUR 7500** (see Figure 2.4) and a **customer discount** (**K007**) in the amount of **20.00%** (corresponding to **EUR 1500**) (see Figure 2.5) were determined, resulting in an invoice sale in the amount of **EUR 6000**.

This pricing is defined in the Customizing for SD; the prices and other conditions can be found in the SD master data. These other prices and conditions are created using transaction VK11:

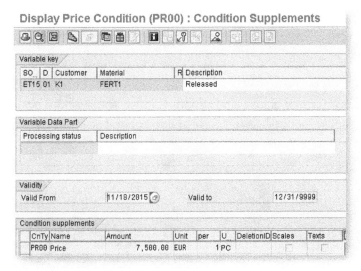

Figure 2.4: Gross list price PR00

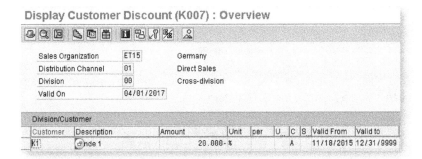

Figure 2.5: Customer discount condition K007

2.3 Revenue and cost collectors?

Do we collect revenues and costs on our sales order? You can recognize this—once you have returned to the overview of your sales order—by switching to COST REPORT in the ENVIRONMENT menu item. If the message ITEM IS NOT RELEVANT FOR COSTS appears, the sales order is neither relevant for costs nor do we collect revenues on it (see Figure 2.6).

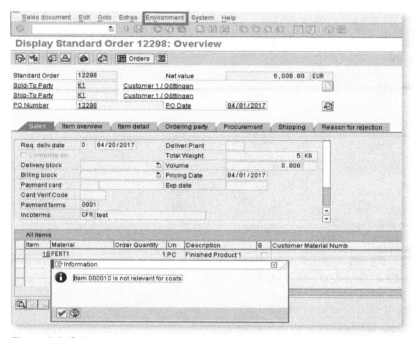

Figure 2.6: Sales order—not relevant for costs

Where is this determined? This is controlled by the *requirements class*, which can also be found in the SD Customizing.

In our sales order overview, let us now go to the PROCUREMENT tab: there, (see Figure 2.7) we can see the *requirements type* **011** for our sales order item.

Figure 2.7: Requirements type 011

In SD Customizing, under SALES AND DISTRIBUTION • BASIC FUNCTIONS • AVAIL-ABILITY CHECK AND PASSING ON OF REQUIREMENTS • PASSING ON OF REQUIRE-MENTS • DEFINE REQUIREMENTS CLASSES, we have defined requirements class **011** and assigned it to requirements type **011** (see Figure 2.8).

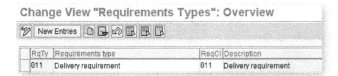

Figure 2.8: Assigning requirements class 011 to requirements type 011

In the requirements class, in the ACCOUNT ASSIGNMENT CATEGORY field, you define whether the sales order is maintained as a Controlling object.

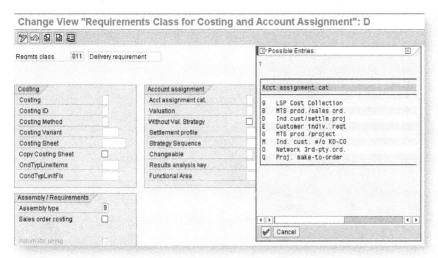

Figure 2.9: Account assignment category in the requirements class

As already mentioned, this is a significant indicator of whether you subsequently transfer the invoices directly to CO-PA. In our example, the ACCOUNT ASSIGNMENT CATEGORY field for requirements class **011** is blank (see Figure 2.9). This means that sales orders that are assigned to requirements class **011** via requirements type **011** do not carry costs and revenues. Later on in the process, this will lead to invoice data being transferred to CO-PA in real time from SD at the precise moment in time when it is saved in the ERP system!

2.4 Interface to CO-PA

In order to be able to transfer sales order data to CO-PA, you have to first allow this in the CO-PA Customizing. To do this, call up the Implementation Guide and via the path PROFITABILITY ANALYSIS • ACTUAL VALUE FLOWS • TRANSFER SALES ORDER RECEIPTS, select the function ACTIVATE SALES ORDER RECEIPTS and in the INC.SO field, enter **1** (see Figure 2.10).

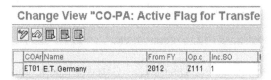

	COAr	Name		From FY	Op.c	Inc.SO	
	ET01	E.T. Germany		2012	Z111	1	

Figure 2.10: Activation to operating concern Z111 in controlling area ET01

Furthermore, value fields in CO-PA must be assigned to the condition types (see Figure 2.11).

Op. concern   Z111   Eifler Company

CTyp	Name	Val. fld	Description	Transfer +/-
B002	⊡terial Rebate	BONUS	Annual rebates	☐
B003	Customer Rebate	BONUS	Annual rebates	☐
FK00	Cust. shipment(IDES)	VV100	Outgoing freight	☐
K005	Customer/Material	RABAT	Other discounts	☐
K007	Customer Discount	RABAT	Other discounts	☐
PR00	Price	ERLOS	Revenue	☐
VPRS	Cost	VV225	Costs of Goods Issue	☐
ZSKT	Cash Discount	VV070	Cash discount	☐

Figure 2.11: Assignment of SD condition types to value fields

Once you have created your sales order (in the example it is sales order **12298**), you have to save it.

We now check in CO-PA whether saving the sales order has actually created line items. You can look at the line items created using transaction KE24. To do this, as shown in Figure 2.12, first set the operating concern before using the green checkmark to access the selection screen for the actual line items of CO-PA (Figure 2.13).

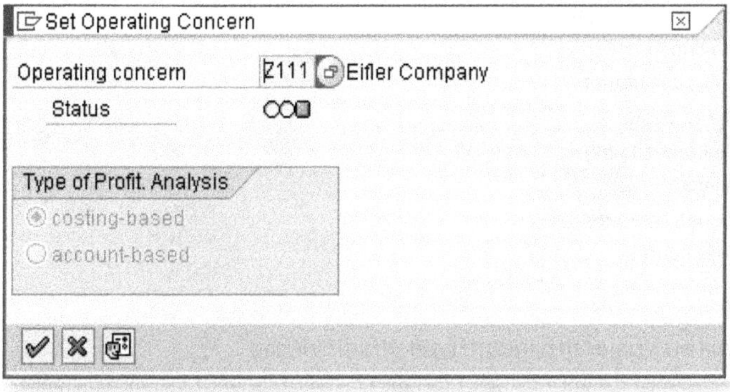

Figure 2.12: Setting operating concern Z111

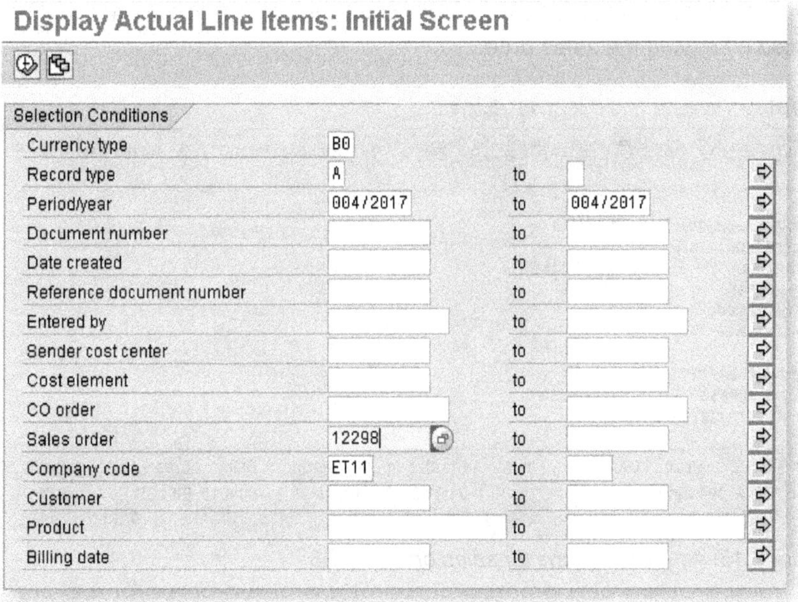

Figure 2.13: Selecting the CO-PA actual line items with transaction KE24

On this selection screen you can see an important characteristic for CO-PA: the *record type*. You can use this to see where the data in your operating concern comes from. Figure 2.14 shows the default values delivered by SAP.

A	Incoming sales order
B	Dir.posting from FI
C	Order/proj.settlemnt
D	Overhead costs
E	Single trans costing
F	Billing data
G	Customer agreements
H	Stat. key figures
I	Order-rel. project

Figure 2.14: Default values of the record type characteristic

If, when executing transaction KE24, you select record type **A**, you can be sure that the ERP system will also only output sales order data.

When we run the selection we see our actual line items (Figure 2.15) that we created by saving the sales order.

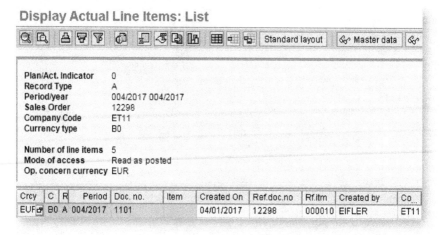

Figure 2.15: Actual line items for sales order 12298

By double-clicking the line item, you can switch between the tabs CHARAC-TERISTICS, VALUE FIELDS, ORIGIN DATA, and ADMINISTRATION DATA (see Figure 2.16 and Figure 2.17). Let us look firstly at the characteristics that were also specified in this line item:

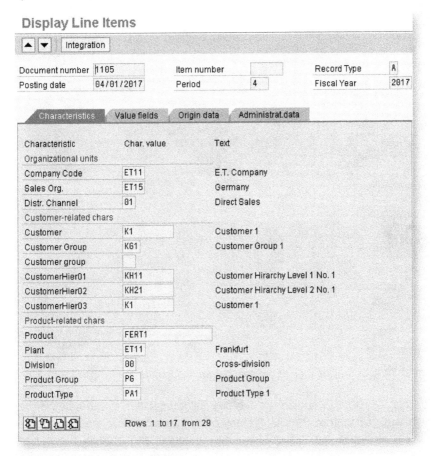

Figure 2.16: Characteristics of the sales order line item I

45

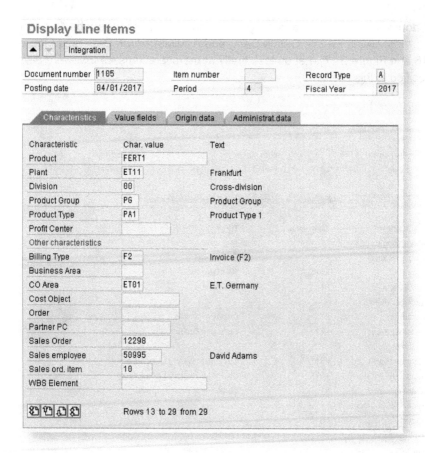

Figure 2.17: Characteristics of the sales order line item II

You can see that in addition to the few fields specified in the sales order, such as CUSTOMER or PRODUCT, many other characteristics are also provided. For example, information from the customer and product hierarchies which you have usually developed from *characteristic derivations* is available. These characteristic derivations are provided via transaction KEDR. In addition to standard fixed derivations, here you can also define free derivations depending on which characteristic of your operating concern is also to be filled.

Value fields have also been filled. You will remember that we specified only quantity information (**1.00** piece of the product **FERT1**), a gross list price **PR00** (**EUR 7500**), and a discount **K007** (**EUR 1500**) in the sales order and nothing more!

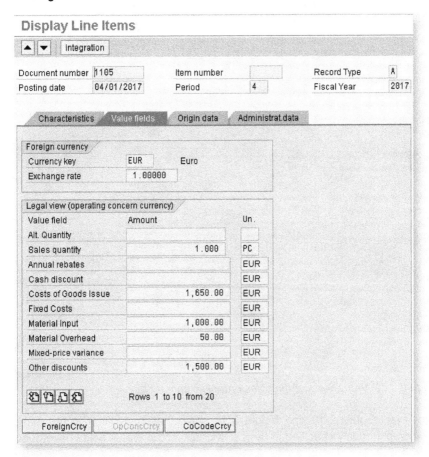

Figure 2.18: Value fields of the sales order line item I

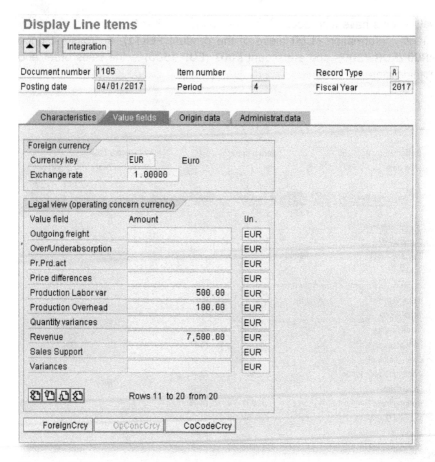

Figure 2.19: Value fields of the sales order line item II

However, Figure 2.18 and Figure 2.19 show that in addition to the information previously specified in the sales order, further value fields have been filled.

Where does this additional information come from? As part of the *valuation strategy* that we defined in the Customizing for our Profitability Analysis, (transaction KE4U), we defined that we wanted to perform material costing for the product we are selling (see Figure 2.20).

| Operating concern | Z111 | Eifler Company |
| Val. strategy | Z01 | Val. Z111 Actual |

Sequence	Appl.	Costg sh.	Description	Mat. cstg	Qty field	Exit no.
1		ⓓ		☑	ABSMG	
2				☐		U01

Figure 2.20: Defining the valuation strategy (transaction KE4U)

Our material **FERT1** was created with material type **FERT** (see also Section 1.2.1). In the next step, as we can see in Figure 2.21, we assign the valuation strategy **Z01** to material type **FERT** (transaction KE4J).

Change View "Costing Key for Material Type": Ov

| 🖉 | New Entries | 🗅 🖫 🖄 🖺 🖺 🖺 |

| Operating concern | Z111 | Eifler Company |

PV	RecT.	Plan ver.	Mat.typ	Valid to	C.key 1	C.key 2	C.key 3
01	A		FERT	12/31/2099	Z01	ⓓ	
01	F		FERT	12/31/9999	Z01		

Figure 2.21: Assigning the valuation strategy (transaction KE4J)

This ensures that the saved adjusted standard cost estimate for product **FERT1** is found and its values transferred to the CO-PA value fields because we have assigned the cost components of the adjusted standard cost estimate to individual value fields in our operating concern **Z111** (see Figure 2.22).

| Op. concern | Z111 | Eifler Company |
| Cost comp. stru | 01 | Product Costing |

PV	CCo	Name of Cost Comp.	F/V	Fld name 1
01	10	Raw Materials	3	VV150
01	30	Production Labor	3	VV180
01	80	Material Overhead	3	VV250
01	120	Other Costs	3	VV255
03	10	Raw Materials	3	VV150
03	50	Production Machine	3	VV180
04	10	Raw Materials	3	VV150
04	50	Production Machine	3	VV180

Figure 2.22: Assigning cost components to value fields (transaction KE4R)

49

If we now compare the values summarized in Figure 1.8 with the information in the value fields of our sales order line item, we can see that the value fields MATERIAL INPUT, MATERIAL OVERHEAD, PRODUCTION LABOR VARIABLE, and MANUFACTURING OVERHEAD contain identical information.

Further information on characteristic derivation and valuation in CO-PA

 You can find an extensive overview with detailed information on characteristic derivation and valuation in CO-PA in Stefan Eifler's book "Quick Guide to SAP CO-PA (Profitability Analysis)" (print version p. 31–75), which is also available from Espresso Tutorials.

Observant readers will of course have noticed that another field, which we have not referred to yet, has also been filled: the COST OF GOODS ISSUE field. This field contains a value of **EUR 1650**. Where does this value come from? Is it simply the total of the value fields that we have used for the adjusted standard cost estimate? If that were the case, it would be too simple and not worth further consideration. No, here we fall back on a standard SAP condition type: the *condition type VPRS*.

To illustrate this, let's go from the CO-PA line item directly to the SD sales order (see Figure 2.24) using the INTEGRATION button (see Figure 2.23).

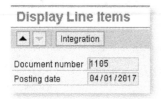

Figure 2.23: Integration of the customer line item with other modules

If we continue from there to the overview of the conditions for the sales order, we can see that the condition type **VPRS** shows a value of **EUR 1650**. To enable this, you have to ensure that this condition type is defined in the SD costing sheet for pricing.

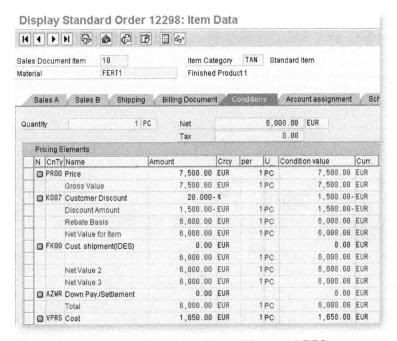

Figure 2.24: Sales order item data with condition type VPRS

As a result of the assignment of the condition type to the COSTS OF GOODS ISSUE value field (see Figure 2.11), **EUR 1650** is now visible in the CO-PA sales order line item.

At this point we must say that the information from this condition type is not that important for the sales order line item yet because we already know what our product is worth from the adjusted standard cost estimate. Nevertheless, during the course of our process, this condition type will become very important because it will provide us with the actual costs of goods issue posted in *Finance (FI)*. This is the only way in a costing-based form of CO-PA to see the actual costs posted in FI and ultimately to ensure a reconciliation of the values between FI and CO-PA up to the operating profit.

As mentioned at the beginning of this chapter, recording a sales order does not yet lead to any postings in FI but, provided the system has been configured in this way, it does lead to CO-PA line items.

What do the value fields of this line item look like in a CO-PA report that you define in the dynamic reporting of CO-PA (details can be found in the above-mentioned book) and run with transaction KE30?

```
Gross Profit

Sales Order Multiple values ⇨
   ┌─Navigation─
   Customer                 ☒ Company Code    ▲ ▼ ⊖ ET11
   Product                  ☒ Sales Order     ▲ ▼ ⊖ 12298
   Sales ord. item

   ≗ ⟳ ✖
```

	Order Intake 04/17-04/17	Actual 04/17-04/17
Quantity	1.000	0.000
Revenues	7,500.00	0.00
Discounts	1,500.00	0.00
Total Revenue	6,000.00	0.00
Cost of Goods Issue	1,650.00	0.00
Production Order Var	0.00	0.00
Materials	1,000.00	0.00
Material Overheads	50.00	0.00
Production	500.00	0.00
Production Overhead	100.00	0.00
Calc. Prod. Costs	1,650.00	0.00
Variance Act vs.Calc	0.00	0.00
Gross Profit	4,350.00	0.00
Assessments	0.00	0.00
EBIT	4,350.00	0.00

Figure 2.25: Presentation of the order receipt in the CO-PA report

In the gross profit structure shown in Figure 2.25, which we announced in Section 1.1.3, you can see an auxiliary line VARIANCE BETWEEN ACTUAL AND CALCULATED COSTS (VARIANCE ACT. VS CALC.). For the order receipt, this auxiliary line still shows a value of **EUR 0.00** because the costs of the goods issue (via VPRS) and the total of the calculated production costs are identical. This auxiliary line is important when the ACTUAL costs of the goods issue that are posted in FI deviate from the values from the adjusted standard cost estimate (= cost-based value) and you still want to reconcile your gross profit 1:1 with FI!

Figure 2.26 shows how the process so far can be represented.

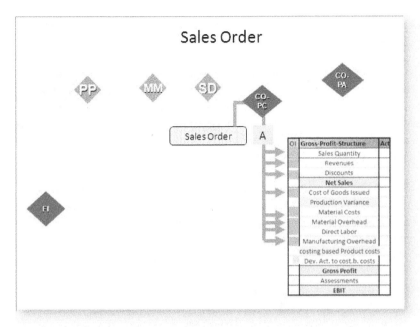

Figure 2.26: Sales order process

1. We enter a sales order in the SD module.

2. When we save the sales order whilst simultaneously considering the adjusted standard cost estimate in CO-PC, the quantity field SALES QUANTITY and the value fields REVENUES, DISCOUNTS, COSTS OF GOODS ISSUED, MATERIAL COSTS, MATERIAL OVERHEAD, DIRECT LABOR, and MANUFACTURING OVERHEAD are filled in Profitability Analysis (CO-PA).

3. In the CO-PA reporting, you can recognize the line items created by the record type **A**. No other SAP modules are affected yet.

All values transferred so far are costing-based, which means that nothing has been posted in FI (which would be more than unusual for a sales order).

2.5 Reconciliation options with accounting

When the sales order is saved (= order receipt), this information is initially transferred only to CO-PA on a cost basis; other accounting modules are not affected at this point. Therefore, we reconcile the order receipt between SD and CO-PA.

Depending on how the SD module is configured, the reporting used in SD can be handled differently in every company. Many companies use the *SIS tool* (sales information system) to present the sales order receipt; some transfer the information from SD to a connected *BW system* (Business Warehouse system) to analyze the information there. For our example, we will use the reports provided in the standard SAP system.

Let us look firstly at a report option in SD. In the application menu, via SALES AND DISTRIBUTION • SALES • INFORMATION SYSTEM • ORDERS, call up the **Orders within Time Period** report. This is a completely normal Report Painter report in SD (see Figure 2.27).

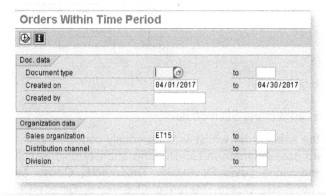

Figure 2.27: Selecting the sales order report

Once you have restricted the period and sales organization and run the report, the list shown in Figure 2.28 appears.

Orders within time period

Dlv.Date	SD Doc.	Item	Material	Description	Order Qty	SU	Net price	Doc. Date	Name 1	SOrg.
**							6,000.00			
*	12298						6,000.00			
04/20/2017	12298	10	FERT1	Finished Product 1	1	PC	6,000.00	04/01/2017	Kunde 1	ET15

Creation Date
04/01/2017 - 04/30/2017   Basic list

Figure 2.28: Result of the sales order report

Another good option for displaying the sales orders in SD is by using transaction VA05N (see Figure 2.29, and as the result, Figure 2.30).

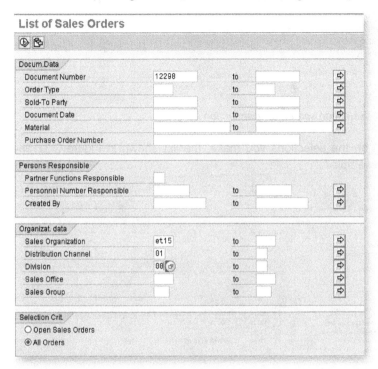

Figure 2.29: Selection screen for transaction VA05N

SD Doc.	TrG	Description	SaTy	Description	Sold-To Pt	Created On	Doc. Date	Pur. Order	Funct	Respons.	Created	SOrg.	DChl	Dv	SOff	SGrp	Curr.	Net value
12298	0	Sales order	OR	Standard Order	K1	04/01/2017	04/01/2017	12298			EIFLER	ET15	01	00			EUR	6,000.00

Figure 2.30: Result of transaction VA05N

You can compare the result with your CO-PA report (see Figure 2.25) and see that the total revenue shown there is identical to the net price of **EUR 6000** shown in the sales order report.

If you want to look at the analysis of the order receipt from the CO-PA side, using transaction KE4TS you can check whether all sales orders have been transferred (see Figure 2.31).

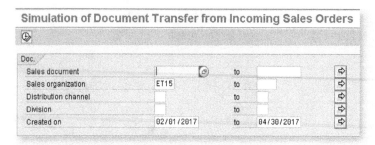

Figure 2.31: Selection screen for transaction KE4TS

Depending on the selections you make, the list shown in Figure 2.32 appears, for example.

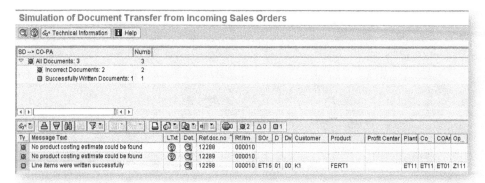

Figure 2.32: Results of transaction KE4TS

The system was unable to simulate the documents marked red at the top; there is a high probability that this sales order was not transferred to CO-PA. The error shown in the MESSAGE TEXT column indicates that there is no material costing for the product to be sold. This material costing has to be created before the corresponding order receipt can be recorded in CO-PA.

However, there might be other reasons why an order has not been transferred to CO-PA; for example, a customer has not yet received a *credit limit release* from **FI**. In this situation, it is quite possible that—depending on how your SD is configured—this order receipt is displayed in SD but not in CO-PA yet. If the customer only receives his credit limit release after the sales order has been created in SD, this order receipt can be found in CO-PA under PROFITABILITY ANALYSIS • ACTUAL POSTINGS • INCORRECT ORDER RECEIPT.

You can use transaction KE2D to display an incorrect order receipt; with transaction KE2B, you can post an incorrect order receipt to CO-PA; and with transaction KE2C, you can delete the order receipt.

Transferring a sales order after going live with SD

 It can make sense to post sales orders once SD has already gone live and you subsequently activate the sales order transfer to CO-PA. This means that in CO-PA, you therefore see order receipts for a period for which so far, sales orders in SD have been posted without an account assignment to CO-PA.

3 The production order

Once the customer has actually made good on his threat and given us an order for our product FERT1, we have to manufacture it. The complete production process is mapped in the SAP module *PP (Production Planning and Control)*. In this chapter, we look at the production process from the financial perspective. We look at the value flows that arise in FI, CO, and CO-PA during the production of our product.

3.1 The standard cost estimate for a production order

Our product **FERT1** is manufactured using a *production order*. All of the procedures associated with the manufacture of our product are mapped to this production order.

The production order contains information about what is produced when and what the final costs of the production order or rather, our product, are.

We create a production order with transaction CO01 (see Figure 3.1). We can display a production order with transaction CO03.

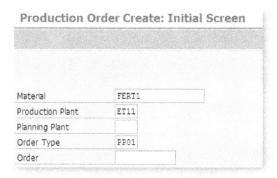

Figure 3.1: Creating a production order

The required entries are the material that we want to manufacture, the plant in which we create the production order or want to manufacture our product, and the order type.

In our case, we manufacture our finished product **FERT1** in plant **ET11** with order type **PP01**.

> ## Order type
>
> Each production order must be assigned to an order type. Certain control information is defined in this order type, for example *number ranges*, the *settlement profile*, or the *functional area* required for managing orders. The order type classifies production orders according to their use.

After we have confirmed our entries, the order header appears. We want to manufacture one piece of product **FERT1**, precisely the one piece that our customer has ordered. Therefore, in the TOTAL QUANTITY field, we enter the production quantity **1**. We also add the start and end time—that is, when production should start and when the product should be completed (see Figure 3.2).

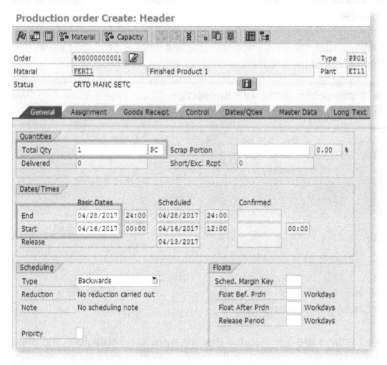

Figure 3.2: Production order header

Once we have entered all this information, we can save our production order. An order number is created.

Costing for the production order

In Customizing, we have defined in order type PP01 that the production order is costed when it is saved—that is, planned costs are costed to the production order as soon as the production order is saved. This means that we do not have to trigger the standard cost estimate for the production order separately.

Via the menu path GOTO • COSTS • ANALYSIS, we can now look at the *cost analysis* (see Figure 3.3).

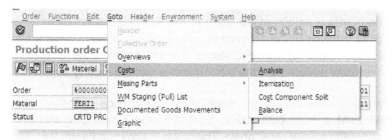

Figure 3.3: Navigating to the cost analysis for the production order

Figure 3.4 shows the cost analysis with the costed planned costs for our finished product **FERT1**.

Transaction	Cost Element	Origin	Origin (Text)		Total plan	Currency		Plan qty
Goods Issues	733331	ET11/RAW_MAT 1	Raw Material 1		400.00	EUR		1
	733332	ET11/RAW_MAT 2	Raw Material 2		600.00	EUR		2
Goods Issues				■	1,000.00	EUR	■	3
Confirmations	943111	KS1/999	Production 1 / Personnel Hours		500.00	EUR		100.00
Confirmations				■	500.00	EUR	■	100.00
Overhead	941111	KS3	Purchase		50.00	EUR		
	941222	KS4	Production Managem.		100.00	EUR		
Overhead				■	150.00	EUR		
Goods Receipt	711111	ET11/FERT1	Finished Product 1		1,650.00-	EUR		1-
Goods Receipt				■	1,650.00-	EUR	■	1-
				■ ■	0.00	EUR	■ ■	100.00

Figure 3.4: Planned costs for the production order

61

We assume that you will recognize the numbers in the TOTAL PLAN column (these are the total planned costs). Exactly: we determined these figures for our product in the adjusted standard cost estimate (see Section 1.2).

The total of the goods issues (consumption of raw materials), the confirmations (labor costs), and the overheads (material and manufacturing overheads) comes to exactly the price of **EUR 1650** for our production material from our adjusted standard cost estimate. The posting of the goods receipt credits the production order with precisely this amount. Therefore, the difference in the TOTAL PLAN column is zero.

Our example could create the impression that the values in the TOTAL PLAN column result from the adjusted standard cost estimate in Section 1.2.2.

This is not correct!

The planned costs are determined again at the time the production order is created, or at the time of the production order costing; they are determined using the *components* and *procedures* of the production order at current prices. These may deviate from the bill of material and the routing.

To illustrate this more clearly, we have changed the price of the material **RAW MATERIAL 1** from **EUR 400** to **EUR 450** (see Figure 3.5) and performed the costing for our order again. The result is shown in Figure 3.6.

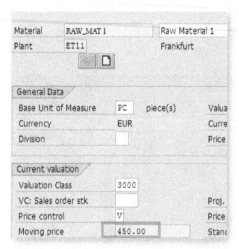

Figure 3.5: Changed price for RAW MATERIAL 1

Plant	ET11 Frankfurt								
Material	FERT1 Finished Product 1								

Planned Quantity 1 ST piece(s)

Cumulative Data
Legal Valuation
Company Code Currency/Object Currency

Transaction	Origin	Origin (Text)		Total plan costs	Currency		Plan qty
Goods Issues	ET11/RAW_...	Raw Material 1		450.00	EUR		1
	ET11/RAW_...	Raw Material 2		600.00	EUR		2
Goods Issues			■	1,050.00	EUR	■	3
Confirmations	KS1/999	Production 1 / Personnel Hours		500.00	EUR		100.00
Confirmations			■	500.00	EUR	■	100.00
Overhead	KS3	Purchase		52.50	EUR		
	KS4	Production Managem.		100.00	EUR		
Overhead			■	152.50	EUR		
Goods Receipt	ET11/FERT1	Finished Product 1		1,650.00-	EUR		1-
Goods Receipt			■	1,650.00-	EUR	■	1-
			■ ■	52.50	EUR	■ ■	100.00

Figure 3.6: Planned costs for the production order: variance

As we can see, the goods receipt still shows our standard price from the adjusted standard cost estimate of **EUR 1650**; however, in the goods issue, the value for **Raw Material 1** has changed from **EUR 400** to **EUR 450** and therefore the material overhead has changed from **EUR 50** to **EUR 52.50** (20% of **EUR 1050**; previously 20% of **EUR 1000**). As already mentioned, this is because in the standard cost estimate for production orders, the current material prices are used.

Planned costs: Standard price

 In the GOODS RECEIPT line, the planned costs of the production order show only the value from the adjusted standard cost estimate or the price determined by the adjusted standard cost estimate from the material master. All components and procedures are revalued with current prices for the standard cost estimate of the production order. For raw materials, there are often variances due to the *moving price* (V price). This price can change every time raw materials are purchased and thus quickly leads to a variance between the current V price and the V price used from the adjusted standard cost estimate.

Now that we have explained and derived the planned costs of our production order, in the following we will continue to work with the original version in which the standard cost estimate of our production order matches the standard price and the adjusted standard cost estimate exactly.

The TOTAL PLAN column is not relevant for our value flow. No values are posted in FI, CO, or CO-PA as a result of the creation of a production order or the creation of the costing. This is also logical because nothing has been manufactured yet, we have only created a costing of the planned costs for our production order.

3.2 Production process

Let us start the production of our finished product **FERT1**. To do this, we have to release our production order using the icon highlighted in Figure 3.7.

Figure 3.7: Releasing the production order

Production can then begin.

We perform the following three steps:

1. Goods issues

We consume the required raw materials for our product FERT1 on our production order with the procedure **Goods issues**.

2. Confirmations

How long did we need to manufacture our product FERT1? We post the working hours performed to our production order. We do this with the procedure **Confirmations**.

3. Goods receipt

After completion, we post our end product to the warehouse using the procedure **Goods receipt**.

We have thus completed the manufacture of our product FERT1. It is now in the warehouse and can be sold.

All three procedures listed above lead to value flows in FI, CO, and CO-PA.

To perform the goods issue posting, the confirmations, and finally the goods receipt posting, we use transaction CO11N (see Figure 3.8).

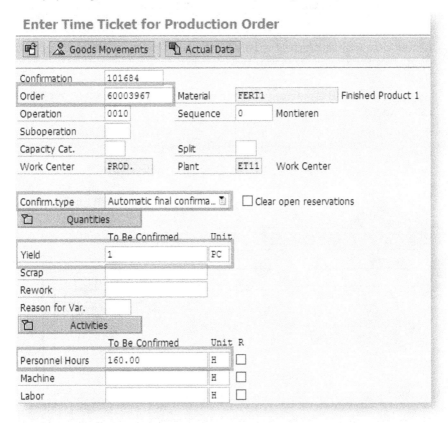

Figure 3.8: Confirming the production order as complete

Transaction CO11N

Transaction CO11N allows you to confirm a production order at procedure level. Therefore, we can use this transaction to post the values and quantities for the raw material consumptions (goods issues), personnel hours (confirmations), and goods receipt postings. The information from the procedures and components of the production order are used as default values. You can change these default values within the transaction, which is what we have done in our example for the personnel hours: instead of using the **100** hours from the routing as a basis, we have increased the personnel hours to **160** hours.

We will now look in detail at what effects goods issues, confirmations, and goods receipts have on our value flow.

Let us look firstly at a diagram of the logistics process (Figure 3.9) to remind you of what we have just described.

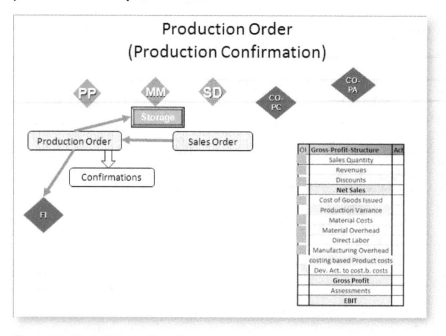

Figure 3.9: Production confirmations

1. The sales order created in the SD module has triggered a production order in PP via the requirements planning.

2. Work takes place on this production order until the employees confirm, via confirmations, that the required procedures have been completed.

3. The product manufactured in production is placed in the warehouse (module MM); at the same time, both the goods receipt for the new product and the goods issues for the raw materials withdrawn are posted in the FI module.

3.2.1 GOODS ISSUES

We will begin with the first procedure, the *goods issues*. For a better understanding, let us call to mind the relevant information from Section 1.2.2: our bill of material for the finished product **FERT1** specifies that we need **one piece** of **RAW MATERIAL 1** and **two pieces** of **RAW MATERIAL 2**, as shown in Figure 3.10.

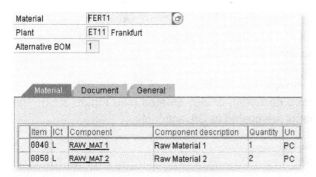

Figure 3.10: Bill of material for FERT1

We will also recall that **RAW MATERIAL 1** has a (moving) price of **EUR 400** per piece and **RAW MATERIAL 2** a (moving) price of **EUR 300**.

In our example, we use precisely the quantity specifications from our bill of material and consume **one piece** of **RAW MATERIAL 1** at a price of **EUR 400** and **two pieces** of **RAW MATERIAL 2** at a price of **EUR 300** per piece.

The confirmations of the material consumptions result in the following three documents:

► Material document

► Accounting document

► Controlling document

The *material document* is created because the **Goods issue** procedure is a goods movement. It is used as information and verification for inventory management. Whenever goods are moved, a material document is created for this movement (see Figure 3.11).

Figure 3.11: Material document

Because these goods movements are movements that are relevant for Finance (FI), an *accounting document* is also created (see Figure 3.12). The corresponding movements are posted to G/L accounts.

Figure 3.12: Accounting document

The G/L accounts posted to are determined via the MM account determination, which is maintained with transaction OBYC, as shown in Figure 3.13 and Figure 3.14. Here we have defined a balance sheet and profit and loss account for the corresponding valuation classes of both our raw materials.

Configuration Accounting Maintain : Automatic Posts - Accounts

◀ ▶ ☐ ☐ ☐ Posting Key ⚖ Procedures Rules

Chart of Accounts	INT	Chart of accounts - international
Transaction	BSX	Inventory posting

Account assignment

Valuation cl..	Account
3000	300000
3001	300010

Figure 3.13: Balance sheet account determination for goods issues

Configuration Accounting Maintain : Automatic Posts - Accounts

◀ ▶ ☐ ☐ ☐ Posting Key ⚖ Procedures Rules

Chart of Accounts	INT	Chart of accounts - international
Transaction	GBB	Offsetting entry for inventory posting

Account assignment

Valuation m..	General mo..	Valuation cl..	Debit	Credit
	VBR	3000	733331	733331
	VBR	3001	733332	733332

Figure 3.14: P&L account determination for goods issues

In the balance sheet, the issue of goods from the warehouse is posted to the stock accounts as a credit. In the profit and loss statement, the expense is posted to the consumption accounts as a debit.

We have defined the valuation class in the material master, as already shown and explained in Section 1.2.1.

Because G/L accounts are addressed in the consumption postings, and we have also created these G/L accounts as cost elements (see Figure 1.6), a *controlling document* is also created for Controlling (see Figure 3.15). The CO object is our production order.

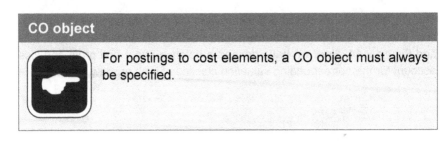

CO object

For postings to cost elements, a CO object must always be specified.

Display Actual Cost Documents

Layout	1SAP	Primary cost posting
COarea currency	EUR	EUR
Valuation View/Group	0	Legal Valuation

DocumentNo Doc. Date Document Header Text		RI RefDocNo User Name Rev RvT		
PRW QTy Object	CO object name	Cost Elem. Cost element name	Val/COArea Crcy	Total quantity PUN O Offst.acct
GO 1702 04/03/2017		R 4900008051 THEIS		
1 ORD 60003967	Finished Product 1	733331 Consump. Raw Mat.1	400.00	1 PC M 300000
2 ORD 60003967	Finished Product 1	733332 Consump. Raw Mat.2	600.00	2 PC M 300010

Figure 3.15: Controlling document

If we now look at the **cost analysis** for our production order, we see that after the confirmations of the material consumptions, in addition to the TOTAL PLAN COSTS column, the first lines in the TOTAL ACTUAL COSTS column also contain entries, specifically, our two material consumption postings, as shown in Figure 3.16.

Transaction	Origin	Cost Element	Origin (Text)	Σ	Total plan costs	Σ	Total actual costs	Crcy
Goods Issues	ET11/RAW_MAT 1	733331	Raw Material 1		400.00		400.00	EUR
	ET11/RAW_MAT 2	733332	Raw Material 2		600.00		600.00	EUR
Goods Issues				▪	1,000.00	▪	1,000.00	EUR
Confirmations	KS1/999	943111	Production 1 / Personnel...		500.00		0.00	EUR
Confirmations				▪	500.00	▪	0.00	EUR
Overhead	KS3	941111	Purchase		50.00		0.00	EUR
	KS4	941222	Production Managem.		100.00		0.00	EUR
Overhead				▪	150.00	▪	0.00	EUR
Goods Receipt	ET11/FERT1	711111	Finished Product 1		1,650.00-		0.00	EUR
Goods Receipt				▪	1,650.00-	▪	0.00	EUR
				▪ ▪	0.00	▪ ▪	1,000.00	EUR

Figure 3.16: Cost analysis for the production order

The raw material consumptions for our production order have created accounting and controlling documents. It is precisely these postings that we show in our FI/CO/CO-PA value flow diagram (see Figure 3.17).

	Finance (FI)		Controlling			
			Cost Center	Production Order	Profitability Object (CO-PA)	
P&L	Value		Value	Value	GP Structure	Actual Values	Cost-Based V.
Sales							
Revenues					Revenues		
Discounts					Discounts		
Inventory Changes					Net Sales	0	
Goods Received FERT							
Goods Received FERT							
Goods Issued FERT					CoS		
Production Variance					Production Variance		
Material Costs							
Consumption Raw Mat.	1000			1000	Material Costs		
Material Overhead					Material Overhead		
Manufacturing Costs							
Direct Labor					Direct Labor		
Manufacturing Overhead					Manufact. Overhead		
Wages Production	1500		1500				
Salary Prod. Mgt.	1000		1000		Gross Profit	0	
Wages Purchase	1000		1000				
Others							
Assessment CCA->CO-PA					Assessments		
EBIT	4500		3500	1000	EBIT	0	

Figure 3.17: FI/CO/CO-PA value flow (I)

3.2.2 CONFIRMATIONS

Again, let us call to mind the relevant information from Section 1.2.2. The confirmations and the personnel costs result from the personnel hours performed multiplied by the underlying activity price. We have planned an activity price of **EUR 5** on cost center **KS1** and activity type **999** with transaction KP26.

As we already know, in the routing for our finished product **FERT1**, we have defined that we need **100 hours** for manufacturing at work center **PROD**. We have also calculated the cost of goods manufactured with these hours.

In our example, for the confirmations of the required working hours, we assume that we need **160 hours** for the manufacture, rather than **100 hours**. Therefore, at this point, we will create a variance to the adjusted standard cost estimate.

Variance to the adjusted standard cost estimate

 In practice, it is normal for actual values to deviate from the adjusted standard cost estimate. Raw material prices can vary constantly during the year, for example, or we simply need more time to manufacture a product.

The confirmations of the personnel hours result in the following three documents:

▶ Confirmation document

▶ Controlling document

▶ Accounting document

As already explained, we have confirmed **160 hours** to the production order. It is precisely these **160** personnel hours performed that we find in the confirmation document (see Figure 3.18).

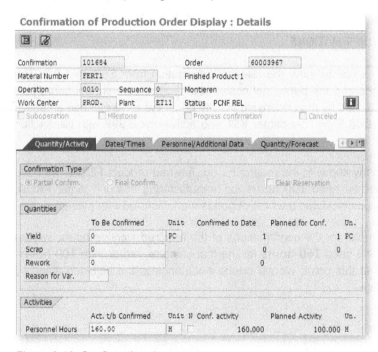

Figure 3.18: Confirmation document

Because the confirmation and the credit to cost center **KS1** and the debit to our production order **FERT1** affect Controlling, a controlling document is created (see Figure 3.19). The posting (also referred to as an *internal activity allocation*) is to secondary cost element **943111—Personnel Hours**. The value of **EUR 800** results from multiplying **160 hours** by **EUR 5** from the cost center activity price planning.

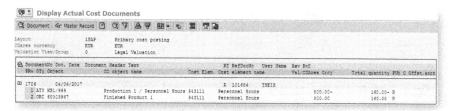

Figure 3.19: Controlling document

You will almost certainly ask why, for a posting to secondary cost elements within Controlling, an FI posting and, accordingly an accounting document are created (see Figure 3.20). The secret behind this is *real-time integration*.

Figure 3.20: Accounting document

In Customizing, we have activated real-time integration in our company code. In our example, we selected the settings such that for secondary postings, an FI document is updated for only selected criteria and not in every case (see Figure 3.21).

Variants for Real-Time Integration CO->FI			
☑ R.-Time Integ:Active Key Date:Active from `01/01/2013`			
☑ Acct Deter.: Active			
Document Type	`AB`		
Ledger Group (FI)	`OL`		
Text	`Real-Time Integration`		

Selection of Document Lines for Real-Time Integration CO->FI			
	☑ Cross-Company-Code	☑ Cross-Profit-Center	
◉ Use Checkboxes	☑ Cross-Business-Area	☑ Cross-Segment	☐ Cross-Cost Center
	☑ Cross-Functionl-Area	☐ Cross-Fund	☐ Cross-Grant

Figure 3.21: Real-time integration

For us, this means that for allocations within Controlling between two Controlling objects with a secondary cost element, postings are created that credit one of the Controlling objects and debit the other object. This generally has no effect for Finance.

However, if an allocation in Controlling leads to a change of functional area, for example (as the FUNCTIONAL AREA column shows in our example in Figure 3.20), this information is forwarded to Finance via real-time integration.

Excursus: Functional area

 A functional area is used to represent the P&L according to *cost of sales accounting*. If you use the *New General Ledger* in FI and have activated cost of sales accounting in Customizing, the functional area is already a fixed component of your analysis options; with the Classic General Ledger, you can map cost of sales accounting in a *cost of sales accounting ledger* or a *special ledger*.

As a result of the real-time integration, all CO documents relevant for Finance are simultaneously transferred to Finance via a *real-time integration account*. The balance of this account is always zero due to the simultaneous debit and credit in Controlling. This means that Finance is always reconciled with Controlling.

Therefore, with our confirmation, an accounting document is created. As a result of the credit to cost center **KS1** with functional area **0110** and the debit to our production order with functional area **0100**, we have created such a change and thus forward the information to Finance.

Avoid posting all CO line items through

 If we select UPDATE ALL CO LIs in the settings for the real-time integration, an FI document is generally created for all secondary CO postings, regardless of whether, for example, there is a change of functional area or profit center or not. Setting this indicator leads to a very large number of FI documents. Therefore, SAP recommends using this setting only for test purposes.

If we look at the cost analysis for our production order again, we will see that there are now more entries in the TOTAL ACTUAL COSTS column: there is an entry in the CONFIRMATIONS line. This is precisely the value that originates from our internal activity allocation of the personnel hours (see Figure 3.22).

Transaction	Origin	Cost Element	Origin (Text)		Total plan costs		Total actual costs	Crcy
Goods Issues	ET11/RAW_MAT 1	733331	Raw Material 1		400.00		400.00	EUR
	ET11/RAW_MAT 2	733332	Raw Material 2		600.00		600.00	EUR
Goods Issues				▪	1,000.00	▪	1,000.00	EUR
Confirmations	KS1/999	943111	Production 1 / Personnel Hours		500.00		800.00	EUR
Confirmations				▪	500.00	▪	800.00	EUR
Overhead	KS3	941111	Purchase		50.00		0.00	EUR
	KS4	941222	Production Managem.		100.00		0.00	EUR
Overhead				▪	150.00	▪	0.00	EUR
Goods Receipt	ET11/FERT1	711111	Finished Product 1		1,650.00-		0.00	EUR
Goods Receipt				▪	1,650.00-	▪	0.00	EUR
				▪ ▪	0.00	▪ ▪	1,800.00	EUR

Figure 3.22: Cost analysis for the production order

This posting also has an effect on our FI/CO/CO-PA value flow (see Figure 3.23). We have credited cost center **KS1** with **EUR 800** and debited our production order with **EUR 800** (**160 hours** multiplied by **EUR 5**).

Finance (FI)		Controlling					
		Cost Center	Production Order	Profitability Object (CO-PA)			
P&L	Value	Value	Value	GP Structure	Actual Values	Cost-Based V.	
Sales							
Revenues				Revenues			
Discounts				Discounts			
Inventory Changes				Net Sales	0		
Goods Received FERT							
Goods Received FERT							
Goods Issued FERT				CoS			
Production Variance				Production Variance			
Material Costs							
Consumption Raw Mat.	1000			1000 Material Costs			
Material Overhead				Material Overhead			
Manufacturing Costs							
Direct Labor		-800		800 Direct Labor			
Manufacturing Overhead				Manufact. Overhead			
Wages Production	1500	1500					
Salary Prod. Mgt.	1000	1000		Gross Profit	0		
Wages Purchase	1000	1000					
Others							
Assessment CCA->CO-PA				Assessments			
EBIT	4500	2700	1800 EBIT		0		

Figure 3.23: FI/CO/CO-PA value flow (II)

3.2.3 GOODS RECEIPT

As described in Section 1.2.2, the goods receipt is always posted to the warehouse at the standard price from the material master. To determine this standard price, we have performed an adjusted standard cost estimate and entered the price determined by the costing in the STANDARD PRICE field in the material master of our production product **FERT1**. Figure 3.24 shows the standard price in the material master of our product **FERT1**. Once production of the product is complete, it is posted to the warehouse.

As a result, we get the following three documents:

▶ Material document

▶ Accounting document

▶ Controlling document

In the same way as for the raw material consumptions on our production order, a material document is also created here (see Figure 3.25)—it is after all a goods movement. Our finished product **FERT1** has been posted to the warehouse and is now waiting to be delivered and invoiced.

Figure 3.24: Standard price for FERT1

Figure 3.25: Material document

The goods receipt posting is also a goods movement that is relevant for Finance. Therefore, an accounting document is created (see Figure 3.26). The goods receipt is posted to G/L accounts.

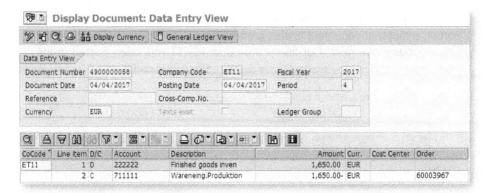

Figure 3.26: Accounting document

In the same way as for the raw material consumptions, the relevant G/L accounts are determined via the MM account determination, which is maintained with transaction OBYC, as shown in Figure 3.27 and Figure 3.28.

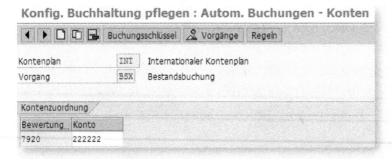

Figure 3.27: Balance sheet account determination for the goods receipt

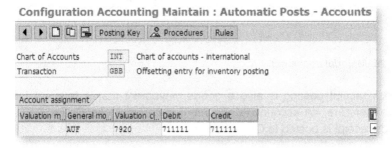

Figure 3.28: P&L account determination for the goods receipt

The goods receipt in the warehouse is posted to the stock account in the balance sheet as a debit. The stock change in the P&L is posted to the consumption account as a credit. We have defined the valuation class in the material master of the respective raw material, as already shown and explained in Section 1.2.1. There, we had assigned valuation class **7920** to our finished product.

The goods receipt posting is a stock change that affects the P&L. We have posted to P&L account **711111** (Finished Product 1), which we have also created as a cost element. As already mentioned, procedures that are relevant for the P&L always have an effect on Controlling. Therefore, a controlling document is created for the goods receipt posting (see Figure 3.29). In this case, our production order is our CO object.

Layout	1SAP	Primary cost posting					
COarea currency	EUR	EUR					
Valuation View/Group	0	Legal Valuation					

🖺 DocumentNo Doc. Date	Document Header Text		RI RefDocNo User Name Rev RvT			
PRw Oty Object	CO object name	Cost Elem. Cost element name	Val/COArea Crcy	Total quantity PUM C Offst.acct

🖙 1722	04/04/2017		R 4900008063 THEIS		
2 ORD 60003967	Finished Product 1	711111 Finished Good 1	1,650.00-	1- PC N 222222

Figure 3.29: Controlling document

Let us look at our cost analysis after the goods receipt posting. As we can see in Figure 3.30, our posting also means that there is now an entry in the GOODS RECEIPT line.

Transaction	Origin	Cost Element	Origin (Text)		Total plan costs		Total Actual Qty		Total actual costs	Crcy
Goods Issues	ET11/RAW_MAT 1	733331	Raw Material 1		400.00		1		400.00	EUR
	ET11/RAW_MAT 2	733332	Raw Material 2		600.00		2		600.00	EUR
Goods Issues				•	1,000.00	•	3	•	1,000.00	EUR
Confirmations	K51/999	943111	Production 1 / Personnel		500.00		160.00		800.00	EUR
Confirmations				•	500.00	•	160.00	•	800.00	EUR
Overhead	KS3	941111	Purchase		50.00				0.00	EUR
	KS4	941222	Production Managem.		100.00				0.00	EUR
Overhead				•	150.00			•	0.00	EUR
Goods Receipt	ET11/FERT1	711111	Finished Product 1		1,650.00-		1-		1,650.00-	EUR
Goods Receipt				•	1,650.00-	•	1-	•	1,650.00-	EUR
				• •	0.00	• •	160.00	• •	150.00	EUR

Figure 3.30: Cost analysis for the production order

The effect of the goods receipt posting on our FI/CO/CO-PA value flow is shown in Figure 3.31.

Finance (FI)		Controlling				
		Cost Center	Production Order	Profitability Object (CO-PA)		
P&L	Value	Value	Value	GP Structure	Actual Values	Cost-Based V.
Sales						
Revenues				Revenues		
Discounts				Discounts		
Inventory Changes				Net Sales	0	
Goods Received FERT	-1650		-1650			
Goods Received FERT						
Goods Issued FERT				CoS		
Production Variance				Production Variance		
Material Costs						
Consumption Raw Mat.	1000		1000	Material Costs		
Material Overhead				Material Overhead		
Manufacturing Costs						
Direct Labor		-800	800	Direct Labor		
Manufacturing Overhead				Manufact. Overhead		
Wages Production	1500	1500				
Salary Prod. Mgt.	1000	1000		Gross Profit	0	
Wages Purchase	1000	1000				
Others						
Assessment CCA->CO-PA				Assessments		
EBIT	2850	2700	150	EBIT	0	

Figure 3.31: FI/CO/CO-PA value flow (III)

The PRODUCTION ORDER column now shows exactly the image that we have just seen in the cost analysis: in addition to the raw material consumptions and personnel costs already posted, we can also see the posting of the goods receipt, which, in addition to the production order, also has an effect on the P&L as an account assignment object in Controlling.

At this point we have reached the end of the production process. Our finished product FERT1 has been manufactured and is now in the warehouse ready for sale.

To complete our production order in terms of costs, we have to perform two procedures which are completed as part of the month-end closing. These procedures are the *actual overhead costing* and the *settlement of variances* for our production order. We will now look at these two procedures in detail in the next section.

3.3 (Month-end) Closing for the production order

3.3.1 Overhead costing

As the first step in the closing process, we perform our overhead costing to debit our production order with the corresponding material overhead and manufacturing overhead costs based on the raw material consumptions and personnel hours posted.

The posting of the *actual overheads* is very clearly CO territory: the actual overheads are triggered actively via the controller. Although the procedures **Goods issue posting**, **Confirmation of personnel hours**, and **Goods receipt posting** that we have posted so far affect the Finance and Controlling areas, they are executed by production employees. We have done this with transaction CO11N.

The actual overhead costing is normally performed as part of the month-end closing for all production orders with actual postings. We too will apply the overhead costing for our production order at this point so that we have then posted all actual costs completely to the production order.

At this point we call to mind some information about the costing sheet from Section 1.2.2 (it is probably slowly becoming clear to you why we were so insistent about the required prerequisites such as the product master data and material costings at the beginning of our book). We had already presented the structure of our costing sheet.

We have defined two overheads: the material overhead and the manufacturing overhead. These are defined as follows:

Material overhead

- ▶ Base: material consumption accounts **733331** (Raw Material 1) and **733332** (Raw Material 2)
- ▶ Overhead rate: **5%**
- ▶ Credit cost center **KS3** (Purchasing)

Manufacturing overhead

▶ Base: account **941222** (Personnel Hours)

▶ Overhead rate: **20 %**

▶ Credit cost center **KS4** (Production Management)

We perform the actual overhead costing for our simple example with transaction KGI2 (Individual Processing of Overheads). This transaction allows us to calculate the overheads on precisely one production order (see Figure 3.32).

Month-end closing of actual overheads

 In the month-end closing, you would not calculate the overheads for each production order individually; instead, you would use mass transaction CO43 (Collective Processing of Overheads). In this transaction, you select the relevant plant and the SAP system calculates and posts the corresponding actual overheads for each relevant production order.

Actual Overhead Calculation: Order

Controlling Area	ET01
Order	60003967

Parameters
Period	4
Fiscal Year	2017

Processing Options
☑ Test Run
☐ Dialog display

Figure 3.32: Transaction KGI2: Calculating the actual overheads

We select our production order **60003967**, specify the relevant posting period and the fiscal year, and can thus run the actual overhead costing. You can run the calculation as a test run first by selecting the TEST RUN checkbox. When you deselect this checkbox, the SAP system posts the corresponding overheads to the production order; or, more precisely, the cost centers defined in the costing sheet are credited and our production order debited with the percentage overhead rate.

Figure 3.33 shows the result of our calculation.

Actual Overhead Calculation: Order Debits

Debits

Senders	Receivers	Cost Elem.	Σ	Val/COArea Crcy
CTR KS3	ORD 60003967	941111		50.00
CTR KS4		941222		160.00
			■	210.00

Figure 3.33: Transaction KGI2: Result of the actual overhead costing

Two lines are shown, whereby the first line shows the material overhead of **5%** on **EUR 1000** raw material consumption and the second line shows the production overhead of **20%** on **EUR 800**.

Let us look at the documents created from this actual overhead calculation:

► Controlling document

► Accounting document

A controlling document is created (see Figure 3.34). According to this document, the overhead costing has an effect on Controlling. As a result of these overheads, our indirect costs such as **Purchase** and **Production Management** are credited to the corresponding cost centers and our production order is debited with the percentage-based overheads. In the same way as for the confirmation of the personnel hours, the overheads are a secondary posting within Controlling. We defined the secondary cost elements **941111** (Material Overhead) and **941222** (Manufacturing Overhead) used in our costing sheet **ZZUSCH** (see Section 1.2.2).

Display Actual Cost Documents

| Q Document | 𝔊 Master Record | | | | | | | | |

Layout	1SAP	Primary cost posting
COarea currency	EUR	EUR
Valuation View/Group	0	Legal Valuation

| 🏠 DocumentNo Doc. Date Document Header Text | | RI RefDocNo User Name Rev RvI |
PRw OTy Object	CO object name	Cost Elem. Cost element name Val/COArea Crcy
🔲 1726　04/04/2017		THEIS
1 ORD 60003967	Finished Product 1	941111 Purchasing 50.00
2 CTR KS3	Purchase	941111 Purchasing 50.00-
3 ORD 60003967	Finished Product 1	941222 Production Manager 160.00
4 CTR KS4	Production Managem.	941222 Production Manager 160.00-

Figure 3.34: Controlling document

As part of our actual overhead costing an accounting document is also created (see Figure 3.35)—again, the same principle applies as for the confirmations of the personnel hours.

Even though this is a secondary CO posting within Controlling, in which in
our example costs centers are credited and production orders debited, there
is also a change of functional area, specifically, from "no" functional area to
functional area **0100**.

Postings WITHOUT a functional area

 Usually, all postings should include a functional area.
The fact that our case involves postings without a functional area is due solely to the example we selected and
the master data settings we defined. A well-known SAP
consultant had only one word for this constellation:
"bad". However, this example also clearly shows the principle because there is a change of functional area that leads to the creation of an
accounting document.

Again, the magic phrase "real-time integration" from CO to FI comes into
play.

Let us look at the cost analysis for our production order again. As we can
see in Figure 3.36, all lines in the TOTAL ACTUAL COSTS column are filled. This
means that all actual costs have been posted to our production order.

Figure 3.35: Accounting document

```
Order            60003967 FERT1
Order Type       PP01 Standard Production Order (int. number)
Plant            ET11 Frankfurt
Material         FERT1 Finished Product 1

Planned Quantity  1 ST piece(s)
Actual Quantity   1 ST piece(s)

Cumulative Data
Legal Valuation
Company Code Currency/Object Currency
```

Transaction	Origin	Cost Element	Origin (Text)	∑	Total plan costs	∑	Total Actual Qty	∑	Total actual costs	Crcy
Goods Issues	ET11/ RAW MATERIAL 1	733331	Raw Material 1		400.00		1		400.00	EUR
	ET11/ RAW MATERIAL 2	733332	Raw Material 2		600.00		2		600.00	EUR
Goods Issues				∎	1,000.00	∎	3	∎	1,000.00	EUR
Confirmations	KS1/999	943111	Production 1 / Personnel ...		500.00		160.00		800.00	EUR
Confirmations				∎	500.00	∎	160.00	∎	800.00	EUR
Overhead	KS3	941111	Purchase		50.00				50.00	EUR
	KS4	941222	Production Managem.		100.00				160.00	EUR
Overhead				∎	150.00		∎		210.00	EUR
Goods Receipt	ET11/FERT1	711111	Finished Product 1		1,650.00-		1-		1,650.00-	EUR
Goods Receipt				∎	1,650.00-		1- ∎		1,650.00-	EUR
				∎∎	0.00	∎∎	160.00	∎∎	360.00	EUR

Figure 3.36: Cost analysis for the production order

We can see that there is a total remaining amount of **EUR 360**. We will see what these remaining costs are and what last steps we still have to perform in a moment.

The overhead costing also has an effect on our value flow (see Figure 3.37). We have credited cost centers **KS3** with **EUR 50** and **KS4** with **EUR 160** and debited our production order with **EUR 50** and **EUR 160** respectively.

Finance (FI)				Controlling			
		Cost Center	Production Order	Profitability Object (CO-PA)			
P&L	Value	Value	Value	GP Structure		Actual Values	Cost-Based V.
Sales							
Revenues				Revenues			
Discounts				Discounts			
Inventory Changes				Net Sales		0	
Goods Received FERT	-1650		-1650				
Goods Received FERT							
Goods Issued FERT				CoS			
Production Variance				Production Variance			
Material Costs							
Consumption Raw Mat.	1000		1000	Material Costs			
Material Overhead		-50	50	Material Overhead			
Manufacturing Costs							
Direct Labor		-800	800	Direct Labor			
Manufacturing Overhead		-160	160	Manufact. Overhead			
Wages Production	1500	1500					
Salary Prod. Mgt.	1000	1000		Gross Profit		0	
Wages Purchase	1000	1000					
Others							
Assessment CCA->CO-PA				Assessments			
EBIT	2850	2490	360	EBIT		0	

Figure 3.37: FI/CO/CO-PA value flow (IV)

3.3.2 Settling the variance

As promised, in the second step we will now clarify and handle the remaining **EUR 360** on the production order. This is the *variance* between our actual costs posted and the adjusted standard cost estimate or the target costs.

Let us look at the current status of the TOTAL ACTUAL COSTS column in our cost analysis in Figure 3.36 again.

On our production order, we have used raw materials to the value of **EUR 1000** and posted personnel hours to the value of **EUR 800** to manufacture our product **FERT1**. In addition, we have debited the production order with material overhead of **EUR 50** and production overhead costs of **EUR 160**. Our actual cost of goods manufactured is therefore **EUR 2010**, precisely the total from the procedures specified.

After completion, we finally posted our product to the warehouse with a goods receipt posting in the value of **EUR 1650**. In Section 1.2.2, we explained why the goods receipt posting is executed with the standard price from the material master, which is **EUR 1650**.

The difference between the actual cost of goods manufactured of **EUR 2010** and the goods receipt posting of **EUR 1650** is precisely the amount that we see on the production order as a difference: **EUR 360**.

We now have to settle this variance between the actual cost of goods manufactured and the standard price in order to completely close the production order.

Both the calculation and the settlement of the variance are—just like the actual overhead costing—pure CO territory and a month-end closing activity within Controlling.

Prerequisites for calculating the variance

To calculate the variance the following prerequisites must be fulfilled:

1. Define the variance key

A variance can only be calculated for a production order if a *variance key* is defined in the production order. We define this using transaction OKV1. The key defines whether, during the variance calculation, *scrap* should be determined and whether *line items* should be updated.

In transaction OKVW, we assign the variance key to a plant. This means that when material master data is created, this variance key is proposed in the costing view. When a production order is created, the variance key from the costing view of the material is then transferred to the production order as the *default value*.

In our example, we created variance key **PP1** (Variance Calculation for Orders) and assigned it to our plant **ET11** as the default value. This means that when we create the material master data for our finished product **FERT1**, the key is defined in costing view 1 and is automatically transferred to the header data when we create our production order (see Figure 3.38).

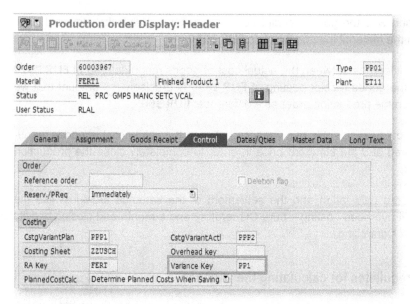

Figure 3.38: Variance key in the production order

2. Define variance categories

We define the *variance categories* in the *variance variant*. The different vari-ance categories structure the total variance according to its source.

The following variance categories are available:

▶ *Input price variance*:
   Difference between the planned and actual prices of raw mate-rials consumed if the V price has changed.

▶ *Input quantity variance*:
   Difference between the planned quantities of raw materials or production hours and the actual quantities required.

▶ *Resource-usage variance*:
   Applicable where different resources are used; for example, a different raw material to the one planned is used.

► *Remaining input variance*:
All other input variances, for example, a difference between the planned and actual overheads if the base has changed.

► *Output price variance*:
Applicable where activity prices that are not calculated via the planned activity price determination were used.

► *Mixed price variance*:
Occurs when the finished material is valued at mixed prices (as part of mixed costing).

► *Lot size variance*:
Results from different lot sizes.

► *Remaining variance*:
For all other variances that cannot be assigned to a category; in particular, if none of the other categories is used.

You define which variance categories are to be used with transaction OKVG (see Figure 3.39). For our example, we use variance variant **STD** with all available variance categories.

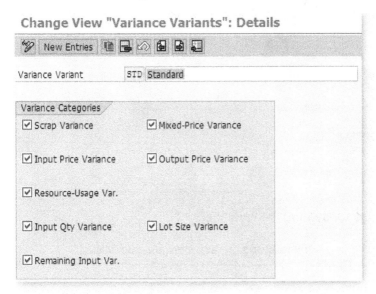

Figure 3.39: Variance categories

3. Define the target cost version

The *target cost version* defines which variance is to be calculated. It controls which costs are to be used as target costs and which costs are to be used as costs to be controlled. You define the version with transaction OKV6. We are working with target cost version **0** (Total Variance). The variance is calculated between the actual costs (costs to be controlled) and the *ongoing standard cost estimate* (target costs), which is the same as the adjusted standard cost estimate we created at the beginning (see Figure 3.40). Our variance variant **STD** is also defined in the target cost version.

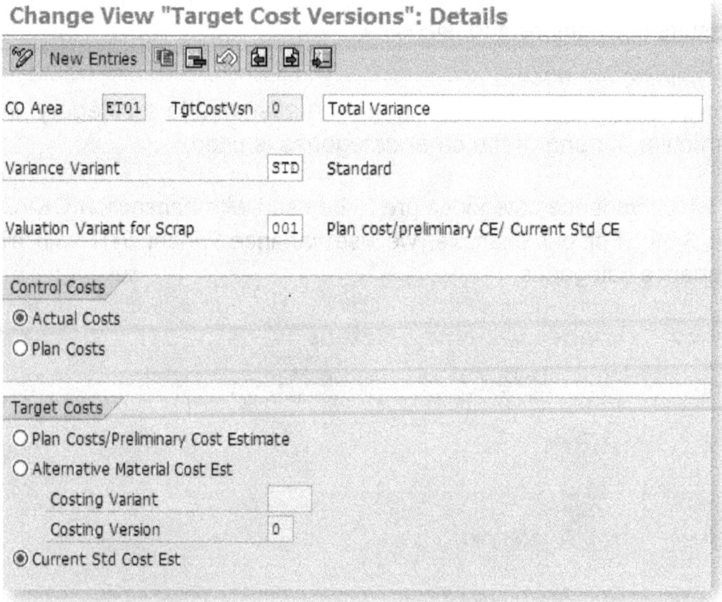

Figure 3.40: Target cost version 0

Prerequisites for settling the variance

To settle the variance, the following prerequisites must be fulfilled:

1. Create the settlement profile

In the settlement profile, we define where our production order is to be settled to. Because we want to settle the variances to CO-PA in our case, it is essential that we allow the settlement of variances in the settlement profile. We define the settlement profile in Customizing via the following path: CONTROLLING • PRODUCT COST CONTROLLING • COST OBJECT ACCOUNTING • ORDER-BASED PRODUCT CONTROLLING • PERIOD-END CLOSING • SETTLEMENT • CREATE SETTLEMENT PROFILE (see Figure 3.41).

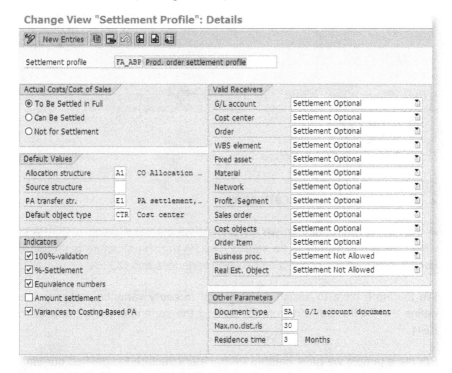

Figure 3.41: Settlement profile for the production order

For our example, we have created the settlement profile **FA_ABP** and assigned it to our order type **PP01**, meaning that this information is automatically transferred when we create the production order.

We assign the settlement profile to the order type in Customizing via the following path: CONTROLLING • PRODUCT COST CONTROLLING • COST OBJECT ACCOUNTING • ORDER-BASED PRODUCT CONTROLLING • PRODUCTION ORDERS • CHECK ORDER TYPES (see Figure 3.42).

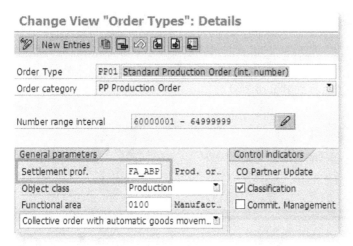

Figure 3.42: Production order type

2. Create the PA transfer structure

In the *PA transfer structure*, we have to define the value fields in CO-PA in which the variances are to be settled. The PA transfer structure is therefore used to establish the connection between variances and CO-PA.

We therefore have to assign a value field to every variance category. We define the PA transfer structure for settling the variances using transaction KEI1.

For our example we have created PA transfer structure **E1**, defined our variance categories as the source, and in turn, assigned a corresponding value field in CO-PA to this source (see Figure 3.43). This PA transfer structure is defined as the default value in the settlement profile.

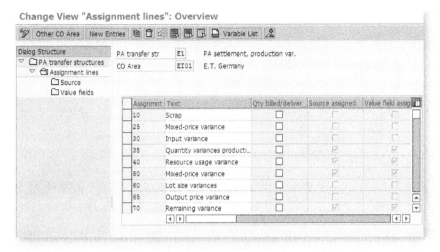

Figure 3.43: PA transfer structure for the production variance

3. Create the allocation structure

In the *allocation structure*, we define which secondary *settlement cost elements* are to be used to settle different *source cost elements* of an order to other *receiver objects*. Because we do not need an allocation structure for the settlement of the variances to CO-PA, we will not go into any further detail here. The PA transfer structure alone is sufficient at this point.

4. Settlement rule

When you create a production order with a valued material, a *settlement rule* is created automatically. This rule states that settlement must be 100% to the material. The second settlement rule (in our case to CO-PA), is created with the first settlement in accordance with the settings in the PA transfer structure. From the production order (transaction CO03), we can display the settlement rule via HEADER • SETTLEMENT RULE. Figure 3.44 shows the first settlement rule for our production order. We can look at the second rule by clicking SETTLEMENT VARIANCES.

Figure 3.44: Material settlement rule

From this screen, we can continue to the *settlement parameters* by clicking GOTO • SETTLEMENT PARAMETERS.

There we see some information maintained automatically via the settlement profile which we need for the settlement to CO-PA. The PA transfer structure is decisive because it establishes the connection between the variance categories and CO-PA (see Figure 3.45).

Display Settlement Rule: Parameters

Order	60003967	Finished Product 1

Parameters

Description		
Settlement profile	FA_ABP	Prod. order settlement profile
Allocation structure	A1	CO Allocation structure
PA transfer str.	E1	PA settlement, production var.
Source structure		
Asset Value Date		
Hierarchy number	0	
Strategy Sequence		

Entered by	THEIS	on	04/03/2017
Last changed by	THEIS	on	04/05/2017

Figure 3.45: Settlement parameters

Calculating and settling the variance

We have thus fulfilled all of the prerequisites for the following in relation to the variance in our production order:

▶ Calculating the variance in the first step

▶ Settling the variance in the second step

We calculate the variance for an individual production order with transaction KKS2. In a month-end closing process, we would use the transaction for processing multiple production orders, which would be transaction KKS1.

We can also perform settlement either for one individual production order or for multiple production orders with the mass transaction. The transaction for individual processing is KO88 and the transaction for mass processing is CO88.

In the same way as for the actual overhead calculation in Section 3.3.1, we perform the variance calculation and settlement with the transactions for individual processing because we are interested in the value flow for our production order.

In the first step, let us calculate the variance for our production order with transaction KKS2. Figure 3.46 shows the selection parameters that have to be maintained.

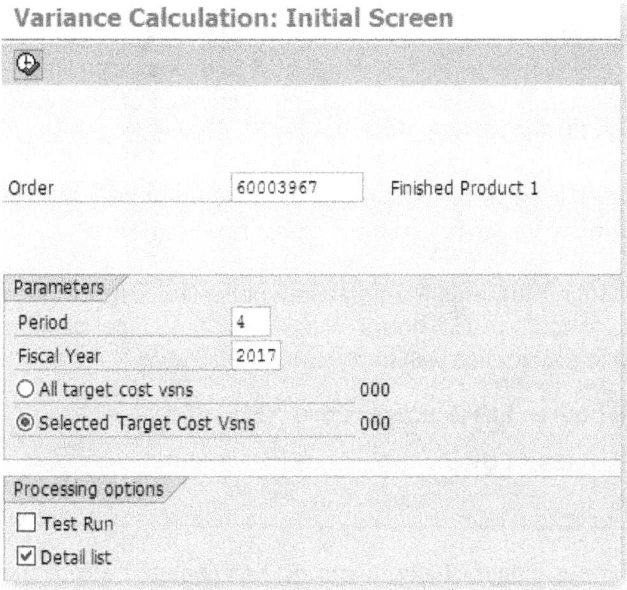

Variance Calculation: Initial Screen

| Order | 60003967 | Finished Product 1 |

Parameters

Period	4
Fiscal Year	2017
○ All target cost vsns	000
◉ Selected Target Cost Vsns	000

Processing options

☐ Test Run
☑ Detail list

Figure 3.46: Variance calculation

With regard to the selection parameters, we specify our production order, the period, and the fiscal year. We also select our target cost version **0**. In the processing options, we can still select the TEST RUN checkbox. If the indicator is not set, the system runs the transaction in update mode immediately. We also select the DETAIL LIST indicator because this triggers the creation of a list with the variances to be posted once the transaction has been run.

After running transaction KKS2, we have the result of the variance calculation for our production order (see Figure 3.47).

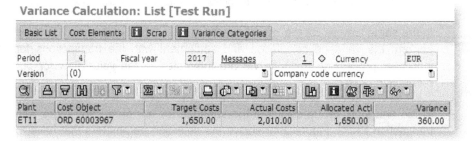

Figure 3.47: Variance calculation

In the list that is displayed we can see some familiar numbers: for our production order, our expected variance amount of **EUR 360** was calculated—the difference between the actual cost of goods manufactured of **EUR 2010** and our target costs of **EUR 1650** from the adjusted standard cost estimate.

In our value flow, the total variance of **EUR 360** is made up of the variance categories **Input quantity variance** and **Remaining input variance**.

Let us recall: we changed the required personnel hours from the planned **100 hours** to an actual figure of **160 hours**. This results in an input quantity variance of **EUR 300** in accordance with the following calculation:

Actual: **160 hours** * **EUR 5** activity price = **EUR 800**

Planned: **100 hours** * **EUR 5** activity price = **EUR 500**

Difference: **EUR 300**

Because the base for our manufacturing overhead has changed due to the increase in the personnel hours, the overhead also changes. Hence our remaining input variance of **EUR 60**, as the following calculation clearly shows:

Actual: EUR 800 personnel hours * **20%** overhead = **EUR 160**

Planned: EUR 500 personnel hours * **20%** overhead = **EUR 100**

Difference: EUR 60

We have now calculated our variance of **EUR 360** and derived the corresponding variance categories.

Now for the second step: settling the variance. To do this we run transaction KO88 (see Figure 3.48).

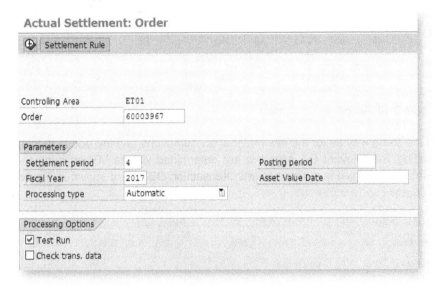

Figure 3.48: Production order settlement

On the selection screen we specify our production order, the settlement period, and the fiscal year.

After running the transaction we have the following documents:

► Accounting document

► Controlling document

► Profitability analysis document

The settlement of the variances produces an accounting document because this procedure has an effect on Finance (see Figure 3.49). There is a posting in the profit and loss statement. A credit variance of **EUR 360** was posted to

97

account **711111** (Finished Good 1). We had already posted our goods receipt of **EUR 1650** to this account (see Section 3.2.3). There was also a debit posting to account **722222** (Price Differences).

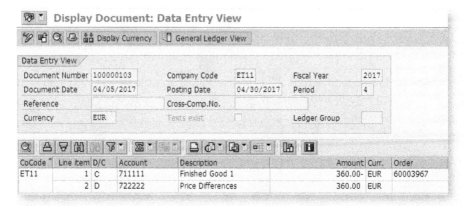

Figure 3.49: Accounting document

In the same way as for the raw material consumptions and the goods receipt posting, the relevant G/L accounts are determined via the MM account determination, which is maintained with transaction OBYC, as shown in Figure 3.50 and Figure 3.51.

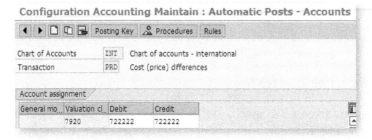

Figure 3.50: P&L account determination for the price difference

For the order settlement, in the account determination for procedure **PRD**, we have defined account **722222** (Price Differences) and for procedure **GBB** (Offsetting Entry for Inventory Posting) and the general modification **AUA**, account **711111** (Finished Good 1). This gives rise to the posting of **EUR 360** for our order settlement.

Configuration Accounting Maintain : Automatic Posts - Accounts

◀ ▶ ☐ ☐ 🖫 Posting Key 👤 Procedures Rules

| Chart of Accounts | INT | Chart of accounts - international |
| Transaction | GBB | Offsetting entry for inventory posting |

Account assignment

Valuation m	General mo	Valuation cl	Debit	Credit
	AUA	7900	711111	711111

Figure 3.51: P&L account determination: GBB-AUA combination

Because procedure GBB is used for multiple procedures which are posted to different accounts (e.g., consumption or scrapping), we have to differentiate these procedures according to a further key: the *general modification*—also referred to as the *account modification*.

Account determination for order settlement

 If the account determination for the combination of "GBB and general modification AUA" is not maintained, the account determination for the combination "GBB and general modification AUF" is used. This combination is also used for the goods receipt posting for the finished product, for example.

The second document created is the **Controlling document** (see Figure 3.52). This document is created because we have created the two FI accounts posted to—**722222** and **711111**—as cost elements as well. Hence this posting also affects Controlling. For the posting to account **711111**, our production order is the CO object. Because we have also created account **722222** as a cost element, the SAP system also requires a CO object for this posting line. In our case, this object is a *profitability segment*. We will explain how this profitability segment is derived and what exactly it is when we look at the documents for Profitability Analysis shortly.

```
⟨⟩ ⁻  Display Actual Cost Documents
Q Document  &↗ Master Record  ◻  Q ▽  ♎ ♎  ▦ ⁼ ⁵   ⍰  ⍰⍰
Layout              1SAP        Primary cost posting
COarea currency     EUR         EUR
Valuation View/Group  0         Legal Valuation
```

DocumentNo Doc. Date Document Header Text		RT RefDocNo User Name Rev RvC		
PRm QTy Object CO object name	Cost Elem. Cost element name	Val/COArea Crcy	Total quantity PUM C Offst.acct	
1731 04/05/2017		R 48560 THEIS		
1 ORI 60003967 Finished Product 1	711111 Finished Good 1	360.00-	S 722222	
2 REC Profit. analysis//E Profitability Analysis	722222 Price Differences	360.00	S 711111	

Figure 3.52: Controlling document

The third document created with the order settlement is the document for **Profitability Analysis (CO-PA)**. If we take another look at all the accounting documents that have been created, we can see that two documents and not just one have been created for Profitability Analysis (see Figure 3.53).

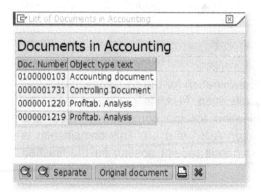

Figure 3.53: Documents in accounting

The settlement of our production order is not only transferred to Finance and Controlling; the variance is also posted to CO-PA.

In our selected constellation we even transfer the variance to CO-PA twice: once as a complete variance of **EUR 360**, and then, in a second document, split into the different variance categories. This is why two CO-PA documents are created.

You will now certainly be asking why we have to settle the variance of **EUR 360** to CO-PA twice. Is it not enough to see it there once?

The question is justified because you do not have to do this double transfer at all. The reason behind it is simply the system settings that we have selected. Let us explain this using the two documents created.

Document 1: Posting of the total variance in CO-PA

We will start with the first CO-PA document (see Figure 3.54). This shows the CO-PA posting of the total variance of **EUR 360**.

This CO-PA posting is created with record type **B**. This is a direct account assignment from accounting.

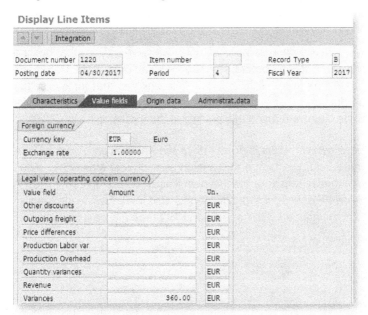

Figure 3.54: CO-PA document: total variance

Let us recall the Controlling document created by the settlement of our production order (see Figure 3.52). Here, the CO object "profitability segment" was posted to for the line of the price difference posting. The profitability segment is the *account assignment object* for CO-PA.

But how is this CO-PA document created?

When we settled our production order we posted to account **722222** (Price Differences). We also created this account as a cost element, which is why it needs a Controlling-relevant account assignment, i.e., a CO object.

In order to specify a Controlling-relevant account assignment for the settlement of cost element **722222**, we use the *automatic CO account assignment* *determination*, which is maintained with transaction OKB9. By doing this we ensure that a CO object is found automatically (see Figure 3.55).

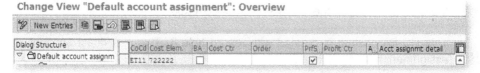

Figure 3.55: Transaction OKB9: price differences

In transaction OKB9, for cost element **722222**, we have defined that posting should be to the CO object "profitability segment" automatically. Hence we selected the checkbox in the **PrfS** column. This ensures that for our settlement of the production order and the FI posting created as a result, a profitability segment is determined and this posting is thus transferred to CO-PA.

So far so good. However, we still do not have the information about the corresponding value field. We define this assignment of cost element to value field in the PA transfer structure for the direct account assignment. The PA transfer structure FI is used for posting costs and revenues to profitability segments and is maintained with transaction KEI2 (see Figure 3.56).

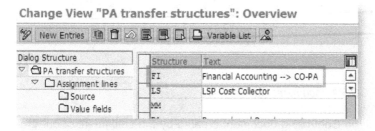

Figure 3.56: PA transfer structure FI

In this PA transfer structure, the corresponding cost element is defined as the source; we have to specify the corresponding value field as the target in CO-PA. Figure 3.57 and Figure 3.58 show the settings for our example.

By assigning the source cost element **722222** (Price Differences) to the value field **VV380** (Variances), in conjunction with the setting in transaction OKB9, we ensure that when our production order is settled, a profitability segment is derived **automatically** for this settlement as the profitability segment, that is, our variance amount of **EUR 360** is transferred to the value field VARIANCES in CO-PA.

PA transfer str	FI	Financial Accounting --> CO-PA
PATransStrAssig	10	Direct costs from FI
CO Area	ET01	E.T. Germany

Cost Element

| From | 722222 | To | |

| Group | | |

Source

⊙ Costs / revenue

○ Variances on production orders
  Variance category

○ Acct. indic. on service orders
  Accounting Indicator

Figure 3.57: PA transfer structure FI: source

PA transfer str.	FI	Financial Accounting --> CO-PA
PA TransStructAssig.	10	Direct costs from FI
Operating concern	Z111	Eifler Company

Quantity/value	F	Value fld	Name	
Value field	3	VV380	Variances	

Figure 3.58: PA transfer structure FI: value field

Price variance via direct posting to FI

 As we already know, we transfer our variance amount to CO-PA a second time when we settle the production order. If you do not want to see this total variance in CO-PA, you can get around this by not defining account **722222** (Price Differences) as a cost element. As a consequence, no CO object would be required for the corresponding posting line and you would not have to set the automatic CO account assignment and the PA transfer structure accordingly.

Document 2: CO-PA posting of the variance categories

Let us take a look at the second CO-PA document created by the settlement of our production order (see Figure 3.59).

This document shows the CO-PA posting of the variance split into the different variance categories. The total of the corresponding value fields is again our total variance of **EUR 360**. This CO-PA posting is created with record type **C**. This is an "order settlement".

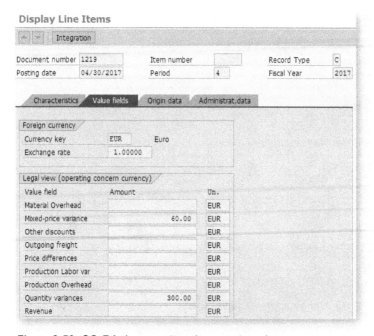

Figure 3.59: CO-PA document: variance categories

Via the PA transfer structure **E1**, the different variance categories are transferred to the corresponding value fields in CO-PA.

Let us look at our cost analysis after the settlement of the variance. As we can see in Figure 3.60, the production order is completely settled.

Our production order is now closed!

Transaction	Origin	Origin (Text)		Total plan costs		Total Actual Qty		Total actual costs	Crcy
Goods Issues	ET11/RAW MATERIAL 1	Raw Material 1		400.00		1		400.00	EUR
	ET11/RAW MATERIAL 2	Raw Material 2		600.00		2		600.00	EUR
Goods Issues			■	1,000.00	■	3	■	1,000.00	EUR
Confirmations	KS1/999	Production 1 / Personnel ...		500.00		160.00		800.00	EUR
Confirmations			■	500.00	■	160.00	■	800.00	EUR
Overhead	KS3	Purchase		50.00				50.00	EUR
	KS4	Production Managem.		100.00				160.00	EUR
Overhead			■	150.00			■	210.00	EUR
Goods Receipt	ET11/FERT1	Finished Product 1		1,650.00-		1-		1,650.00-	EUR
Goods Receipt			■	1,650.00-	■	1-	■	1,650.00-	EUR
Settlement		(without origin)		0.00				360.00-	EUR
Settlement			■	0.00			■	360.00-	EUR
			■ ■	0.00	■ ■	160.00	■ ■	0.00	EUR

Figure 3.60: Cost analysis

To complete our production process let us look at the value flow again (see Figure 3.61).

Finance (FI)			Controlling				
			Cost Center	Production Order	Profitability Object (CO-PA)		
P&L	Value		Value	Value	GP Structure	Actual Values	Cost-Based V.
Sales							
Revenues					Revenues		
Discounts					Discounts		
Inventory Changes					Net Sales	0	
Goods Received FERT	-1650			-1650			
Goods Received FERT	-360						
Goods Issued FERT					CoS		
Production Variance	360				-360 Production Variance	360	
Material Costs							
Consumption Raw Mat.	1000				1000 Material Costs		
Material Overhead			-50		50 Material Overhead		
Manufacturing Costs							
Direct Labor			-800		800 Direct Labor		
Manufacturing Overhead			-160		160 Manufact. Overhead		
Wages Production	1500		1500				
Salary Prod. Mgt.	1000		1000		Gross Profit	360	
Wages Purchase	1000		1000				
Others							
Assessment CCA->CO-PA					Assessments		
EBIT	2850		2490	0	EBIT	360	

Figure 3.61: FI/CO/CO-PA value flow (V)

With the settlement of the variance we have created a posting in the P&L. With this FI posting, the goods received account for finished products was adjusted by **EUR 360** to the actual costs of **EUR 2010** (total of **Goods Recei-**

ved FERT in Figure 3.61). The offsetting entry is to account **722222** (Price Differences).

Our production order was credited with **EUR 360** and is thus completely settled. The corresponding debit was posted to CO-PA.

Here too we want to provide you with a simple illustration of what you have read (see Figure 3.62).

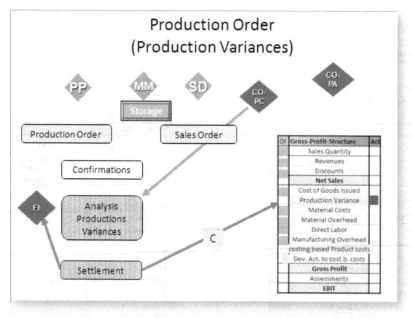

Figure 3.62: Production variance

1. At the end of the period, a production variance calculation is performed from the module Product Cost Controlling (CO-PC).

2. In the subsequent settlement, the production variance is posted to FI and transferred to Profitability Analysis (CO-PA) with record type **C**.

3. The PRODUCTION VARIANCE value field is thus filled.

3.4 Reconciliation options with accounting

As shown in our value flow (Figure 3.61), production variances are calculated and settled as part of month-end closing. Postings in FI and CO-PA are created in this process.

In FI, for example, you can use transaction FAGLL03 (G/L Account Line Item Display G/L View). We select our price difference account **722222** (which we defined in the account determination [transaction OBYC]) and the corresponding posting period (see Figure 3.63).

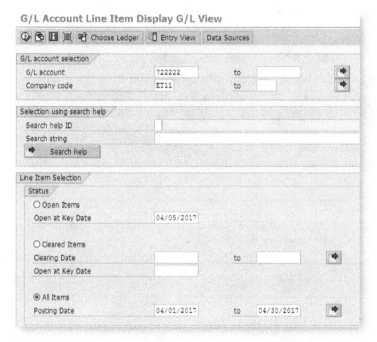

Figure 3.63: Selection screen for transaction FAGLL03

With a useful layout and a suitable filter, you should get to the corresponding variance total in FI (see Figure 3.64).

G/L Account Line Item Display G/L View

G/L Account 722222 Price Differences
Company Code ET11
Ledger   0L

	St	Assignment	DocumentNo	BusA	Typ	Doc..Date	PK	Amount in local cur.	LCurr	Text
☐	✓	60003967	100000103		SA	04/05/2017	83	360.00	EUR	ORD 60003967
•	✓							360.00	EUR	
••	Account 722222							360.00	EUR	

Figure 3.64: FAGLL03: price difference

Suitable filter

 Price differences can of course result from other procedures and be posted to the price difference account. Therefore, it is advisable to design and save a layout that you can call up every month to specifically reconcile the variance from the order settlement. In our case, we set a filter on the ASSIGNMENT column and selected **All Production Orders**.

In CO-PA, we can display our CO-PA report with transaction KE30 to check the variance in CO-PA (see Figure 3.65).

	Order Intake 04/17-04/17	Actual 04/17-04/17
Quantity	1.000	1.000
Revenues	7,500.00	7,500.00
Discounts	1,500.00	1,500.00
Total Revenue	6,000.00	6,000.00
Cost of Goods Issue	1,650.00	1,650.00
Production Order Var	0.00	360.00
Materials	1,000.00	1,000.00
Material Overheads	50.00	50.00
Production	500.00	500.00
Production Overhead	100.00	100.00
Calc. Prod. Costs	1,650.00	1,650.00
Variance Act vs.Calc	0.00	0.00
Gross Profit	4,350.00	3,990.00
Assessments	0.00	0.00
EBIT	4,350.00	3,990.00

Figure 3.65: CO-PA report

Furthermore, in CO-PA, just like in FI, we can use the CO-PA actual line item report (transaction KE24) (see Figure 3.66).

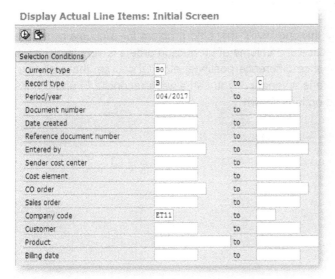

Figure 3.66: Selection screen for transaction KE24

To run the report we select the currency type, the record type, the period, the fiscal year, and the company code. Figure 3.67 shows the result.

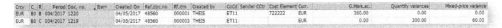

Crcy	C	R	Period	Doc. no.	Item	Created On	Ref.doc.no	Rf.itm	Created by	CoCd	Sender CCtr	Cost Element	Curr.	G.Mark.ac.	Quantity variances	Mixed-price variance
EUR	B0	B	004/2017	1220		04/05/2017	48560	000001	THEIS	ET11		722222	EUR	360.00	0.00	0.00
EUR	B0	C	004/2017	1219		04/05/2017	48560	000003	THEIS	ET11			EUR	0.00	300.00	60.00

Figure 3.67: Results for transaction KE24

Let us call to mind our value flow. We have transferred the variance to CO-PA twice:

▶ Once via the settlement and hence with record type **C**

▶ Once with the posting with cost element **722222** (Price Differences) and the automatic account assignment with record type **B**.

It is precisely these postings that we can display in the line item report. You can design the layout according to your requirements in terms of which value fields and characteristics you want to see in the line item report.

The reports shown are only an example of how we can reconcile the values in FI and CO-PA in the variance calculation. In SAP ERP, there are a number of other reports and reconciliation options.

You are now surely thinking "Well, that's no problem for a couple of simple examples but in practice, the volume of production orders is very large, there is a wide variety of price difference postings, etc." Of course, that's all true. Nevertheless, if there is a variance, you can always reconcile FI and CO-PA with the reports and options shown.

4 Goods issue

We have now successfully manufactured our product FERT1. Think back to Chapter 2, where we described how to create a sales order and what the corresponding connections to accounting look like. In this chapter, we deliver the sales order created.

To do this, we use transaction VA02 to access our sales order again (Figure 4.1).

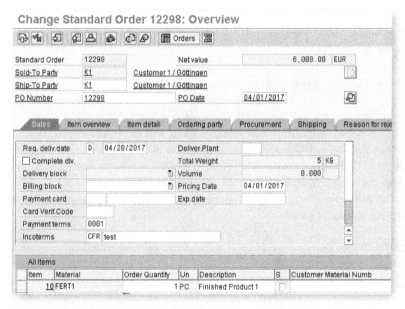

Figure 4.1: Changing a sales order

Via the menu SALES DOCUMENT • DELIVER, we go straight to the delivery (see Figure 4.2).

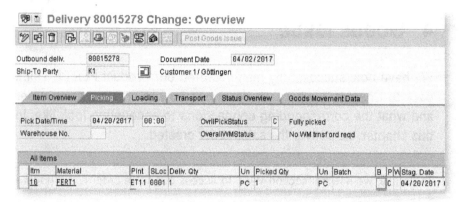

Figure 4.2: Creating a delivery

Once we have entered the quantity to be picked, in this simple example we click POST GOODS ISSUE.

In an ideal situation, the message DELIVERY.... SAVED appears.

You will now say: "It's that easy?" In our example system it is, but in the real world it is somewhat more complicated. At this point we would like to remind you that in this book, the intention is to describe the basic value flow and its effects on accounting (FI, CO, CO-PA). We neither want nor are able to describe all the logistical fine details that are possible for a delivery or a goods issue. We are now interested in what happens in accounting once we have created the message above.

Therefore, in the delivery we have just created, we use transaction VL03N and via the path ENVIRONMENT • DOCUMENT FLOW (or by pressing F7), we look at the document flow (see Figure 4.3).

Document Flow

| 🔍 | ⬛ Status overview | 👓 Display document | Service documents | 🔳 |

Business partner K1 Customer 1
Material   FERT1

Document	Quantity	Unit	Ref. value	Currency	On	Status
▽ 🗋 ➡ Standard Order 0000012298 / 10	1	PC	6,000.00	EUR	04/01/2017	Completed
▽ 🗋 Delivery 0080015278 / 10	1	PC			04/02/2017	Completed
🗋 Picking request 20170402 / 10	1	PC			04/02/2017	Completed
🗋 GD goods issue:delvy 4900008041 / 1	1	PC	1,650.00	EUR	04/02/2017	complete

Figure 4.3: Document flow for delivery

From the sales order, we have created the delivery and are now looking at the goods issue document **GD** in more detail via DISPLAY DOCUMENT (see Figure 4.4).

Figure 4.4: Goods issue document

We are interested (of course) in the accounting documents, and therefore we click ACCOUNTING DOCUMENTS and in Figure 4.5, display the accounting document for the goods issue.

Figure 4.5: Accounting document for the goods issue

Our stock account **222222** has reduced by **EUR 1650** and we have posted the expense of the same amount to the stock change account **893015**. Where did the SAP system get the value for this posting?

In our example, the system used the value at which our product was valued in the balance sheet. As you learned in Section 1.2, our sales products are costed. In a first step, an adjusted standard cost estimate is created and then held and subsequently released. When the adjusted standard cost estimate is released, the standard price (S price) is updated in the ACCOUNT-

ING 1 view of the product master and at the same time, existing stock is re-valued for accounting purposes (see Figure 4.6).

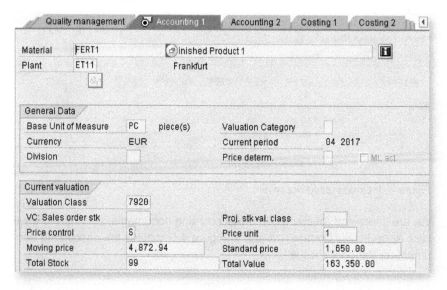

Figure 4.6: Material master: Accounting 1 view

In our example, our sales product is valued with a standard price of **EUR 1650**. We have **99 pieces** of the product in the warehouse, and there-fore we currently report a total stock value of **EUR 163,350** in the financial statements.

With the goods issue we therefore initially have a pure FI posting—nothing has happened (yet) in CO or CO-PA.

How did our SAP system know which accounts to post to? Again, looking at the material master can help us here. In Figure 4.6 we see valuation class **7920**. The valuation class controls the MM account determination (see Sec-tion 1.2.1). If we look at the MM account determination with transaction OBYC, you will initially see a list of MM procedures (Figure 4.7) which have an accounting effect and for which accounts must be defined.

For procedure **BSX** (Inventory Posting) and valuation class **7920**, account **222222** from our chart of accounts **INT** is defined (see Figure 4.8). The counterpart to this is procedure **GBB** (Offsetting Entry for Inventory Posting) for which the stock change account must be defined (see Figure 4.9).

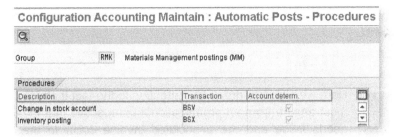

Configuration Accounting Maintain : Automatic Posts - Procedures

Group   RMK   Materials Management postings (MM)

Procedures

Description	Transaction	Account determ.
Change in stock account	BSV	☑
Inventory posting	BSX	☑

Figure 4.7: MM account determination I

Chart of Accounts	INT	Chart of accounts - international
Transaction	BSX	Inventory posting

Account assignment

Valuation cl	Account
7920	222222

Figure 4.8: MM account determination II

Chart of Accounts	INT	Chart of accounts - international
Transaction	GBB	Offsetting entry for inventory posting

Account assignment

Valuation	General m	Valuation cl	Debit	Credit
	VAX	7920	893010	893010
	VAY	7920	893015	893015

Figure 4.9: MM account determination III

We have to be careful now because here the famous *account grouping code* takes effect! For our example we differentiate between two cases: the general modifications **VAX** and **VAY**. Normally, we create P&L accounts as cost elements in Controlling; in this case, however, we do not do that because otherwise we would report the stock change twice in CO: once in cost center accounting, for example (if you had assigned a cost center to the cost element as an automatic account assignment via transaction OKB9), and once because the costs of the goods issue are transferred to CO-PA via the condition type **VPRS** and even statistically via the adjusted standard cost estimate.

These costs would then be in CO-PA twice at the latest after the cost center assessment.

Goods issue and invoice in the same period

Here we explicitly draw your attention to the fact that you must ensure from an organizational perspective that the goods issue and the associated invoice occur in the same period. As we will explain in the next section, the goods issue costs are transferred to CO-PA with the invoice. If the actual goods issue takes place in period 1 and the associated invoice is issued in period 2, you have a difference between FI and CO-PA in both periods!

In summary, our value flow is now as shown in Figure 4.10. The change highlighted reflects the accounting postings in this chapter.

Finance (FI)		Controlling				
		Cost Center	Production Order	Profitability Object (CO-PA)		
P&L	Value	Value	Value	GP Structure	Actual Values	Cost-Based V.
Sales						
Revenues				Revenues		
Discounts				Discounts		
Inventory Changes				Net Sales	0	
Goods Received FERT	-1650		-1650			
Goods Received FERT	-360					
Goods Issued FERT	1650			CoS		
Production Variance	360			-360 Production Variance	360	
Material Costs						
Consumption Raw Mat.	1000			1000 Material Costs		
Material Overhead		-50		50 Material Overhead		
Manufacturing Costs						
Direct Labor		-800		800 Direct Labor		
Manufacturing Overhead		-160		160 Manufact. Overhead		
Wages Production	1500	1500				
Salary Prod. Mgt.	1000	1000		Gross Profit	360	
Wages Purchase	1000	1000				
Others						
Assessment CCA->CO-PA				Assessments		
EBIT	4500	2490	0	EBIT	360	

Figure 4.10: FI/CO/CO-PA value flow (VI)

As part of the logistical process, the goods issue can be clearly represented in graphical form (Figure 4.11):

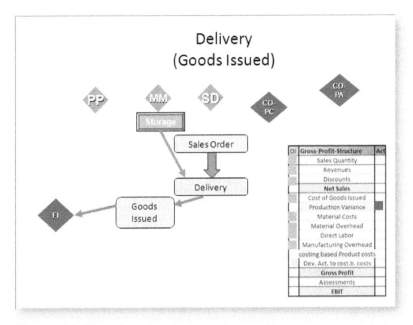

Figure 4.11: Goods issue process

1. In SD, a delivery is created from the sales order; the product to be sold is removed from the warehouse.

2. At the end of the delivery to SD, we click POST GOODS ISSUE to post the goods issue to the FI module.

3. The SAP system notes these actual costs of the goods issue and reports them correctly later in condition type VPRS as part of the invoice.

In all the other modules shown in the graphic nothing else happens yet.

We will look at the topic of reconciliation options with accounting on goods issue in detail in Section 5.4.3.

5 The invoice

The finished goods are on their way to the customer or may already have arrived. We should now send the associated invoice as quickly as possible.

5.1 Creating an invoice

We use transaction VF01 to create the invoice (sometimes also referred to in the SAP system as a "billing document"). Figure 5.1 shows the initial screen.

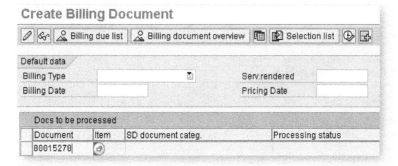

Figure 5.1: Initial screen for creating an invoice

In doing so, we refer to the delivery described in the previous chapter. Before we post the invoice, we look firstly at the header data defined that will appear on the invoice (Figure 5.2), and secondly at the conditions (Figure 5.3) in the item data, which are important for our accounting.

Figure 5.2: Invoice header data

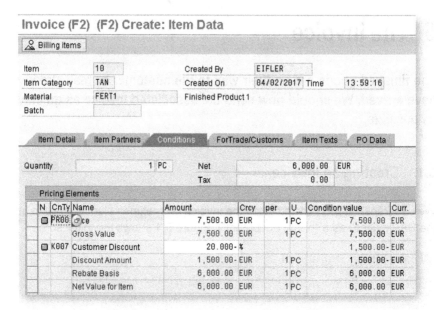

Figure 5.3: Invoice conditions I

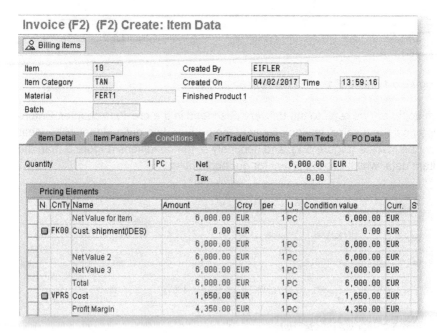

Figure 5.4: Invoice conditions II

You can theoretically still change the gross list price or the discount conditions in the conditions if you have agreed this with your customer after receiving the sales order. We can see, as already described in Section 2.2, that a gross list price **PR00** in the amount of **EUR 7500** and a discount **K007** of **20%** of the gross sales were found.

Figure 5.4 shows that if we scroll down in this condition list, further conditions are displayed.

5.2   Condition type VPRS

In this section we focus on the condition type VPRS delivered by SAP as standard. It reflects the costs of the goods issue actually posted in FI. In the previous chapter, we had recorded goods issue costs in the amount of **EUR 1650** and it is precisely this value that is now shown as the condition value in condition type **VPRS** (Figure 5.4).

So the invoice is looking pretty good. We save, and hopefully the message DOCUMENT ... SAVED appears. If this message does appear, the invoice was posted in accounting in parallel. If the message does not appear, the system advises you that the invoice still has to be released to accounting (and thus also to CO and CO-PA). However, we were lucky and let's now take a look at the accounting documents because that is the only thing we are interested in at this point (start with transaction VF03, see Figure 5.5).

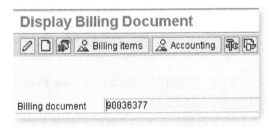

Figure 5.5: Displaying an invoice: initial screen

121

5.3   Interface to accounting

Figure 5.6 lists the accounting documents created.

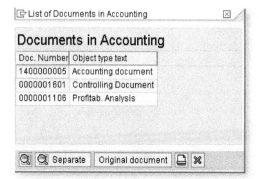

Figure 5.6: Invoice documents created

Profitability Analysis document

Why do you now see a document for Profitability Analysis? You see this document because in Customizing, as described in Section 2.3, you have configured the associated requirements class in the sales order item such that you transfer the invoice to CO-PA directly and in real time. Otherwise you would have first collected these revenues on the sales order which you would later have had to settle to CO-PA, at the latest at the end of the month.

Accounting document

For the purpose of simplification, for the accounting document (see Figure 5.7) we will not consider tax on sales/purchases.

The revenues were posted to account **600000** and the discount to account **600001**. How did the SAP system find these accounts? This is controlled in the Customizing for SD via the SD account determination. You can access this in the configuration menu via SALES AND DISTRIBUTION • BASIC FUNCTIONS • REVENUE ACCOUNT DETERMINATION • ASSIGN G/L ACCOUNTS.

Data Entry View					
Document Number	1400000005	Company Code	ET11	Fiscal Year	2017
Document Date	04/02/2017	Posting Date	04/02/2017	Period	4
Reference	0090036377	Cross-Comp.No.			
Currency	EUR	Texts exist	☐	Ledger Group	

C...	Itm	P	S	Account	Description	Amount	Curr.	Tx	Cost Ce
ET11	1	01		C 1	Customer 1	6,000.00	EUR		
	2	50		600000	Umsatzerlöse	7,500.00-	EUR		
	3	40		600001	Erlösschmälerung	1,500.00	EUR		

Figure 5.7: FI invoice document

For G/L account **600000**, we have configured the settings shown in Figure 5.8.

Change View "General": Overview

New Entries

General					
App	CndTy.	ChAc	SOrg.	G/L Account	Provision acc.
V	KOFI	INT	CPF2	800000	
V	KOFI	INT	ET15	600000	

Figure 5.8: Revenue account determination I

Because G/L account **600000** is assigned to sales organization **ET15**, chart of accounts **INT**, costing type **KOFI**, and the application **V** (Sales and Distribution), it is found for the G/L account posting. You can also maintain this setting at a more specialized level (with no limits to your imagination).

Change View "Cust.Grp/MaterialGrp/AcctKey"

New Entries

Cust.Grp/MaterialGrp/AcctKey								
App	CndTy.	ChAc	SOrg.	AAG	AAG	ActKy	G/L Account	Provision
V	KOFI	INT	ET15	01	01	ERF	800000	
V	KOFI	INT	ET15	01	01	ERL	600000	
V	KOFI	INT	ET15	01	01	ERS	600001	

Figure 5.9: Revenue account determination II

In Figure 5.9, the ACTKY (account key) column is important. **ERL** stands for revenues and **ERS** for sales deductions. You can use this account key to configure the G/L account determination even more precisely.

Create G/L accounts as cost elements!

What is important is that these accounts must be created not only in your chart of accounts and company code; to enable you to also create postings in CO-PA, the accounts must be created as cost elements of type 11 (revenue element) or type 12 (sales deduction).

Controlling document

A second document was posted with the invoice: the Controlling document (see Figure 5.10).

```
▣▣  Display Actual Cost Documents

🔍 Document  | 𝒶ʳ Master Record | ▣  🔍 ▽ : ▣ ▽ | ▦ ◦ ▫ | 🔢 | 🔠 ▣

Layout                  1SAP        Primary cost posting
COarea currency         EUR         EUR
Valuation View/Group    0           Legal Valuation

▲ DocumentNo Doc. Date  Document Header Text                            RT RefDocNo    User Name  Rev RvD
  PRw OTy Object                      CO object name        Cost Elem. Cost element name          Val/COArea Crcy

▣ 1601       04/02/2017                                                 R  90036377    EIFLER
    1 REO Profit. analysis//E.. Profitability Analysis      600000                                        7,500.00-
    2 REO Profit. analysis//E.. Profitability Analysis      600001                                        1,500.00
```

Figure 5.10: Controlling document

This document is created because we have created both FI accounts posted to—**600000** and **600001**—as cost elements as well. Hence this posting also affects Controlling. For both posting lines, a profitability segment is selected as the CO object. We now come to the third document, the Profitability Analysis document.

Profitability Analysis document

Let us look at the line item in CO-PA which was created by the invoice. Because we have not made any change to the original sales order in the invoice, the sales order line item and the invoice line item in CO-PA look very similar. However, we can differentiate them by the record type characteristic: here, the sales order had the characteristic value **A** (see Figure 2.16), and the invoice (Figure 5.11) has record type **F**.

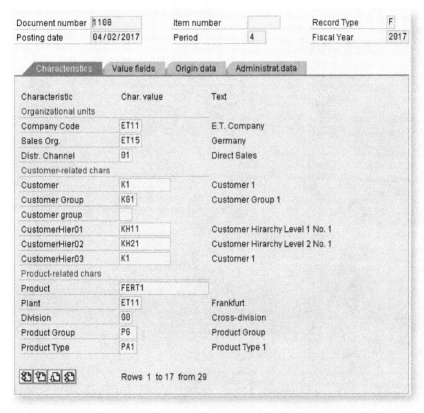

Figure 5.11: Characteristics of the invoice line item I

Furthermore, in this line item, you can see that the original reference to the sales order has been retained, meaning that in a CO-PA report, you will find this invoice line item on the SALES ORDER characteristic **12298** (see Figure 5.12).

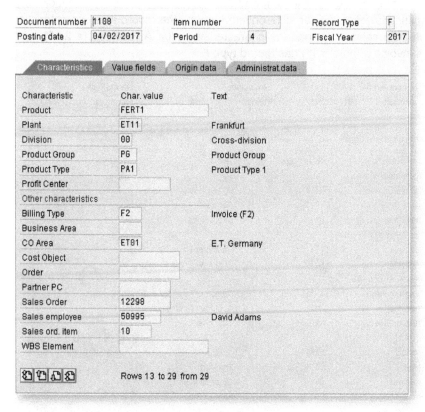

Figure 5.12: Characteristics of the invoice line item II

The invoice condition types PR00 and K007 were transferred to the value fields OTHER DISCOUNTS (Figure 5.13) and REVENUE (Figure 5.14). Condition type VPRS was transferred to the value field COST OF GOODS ISSUE.

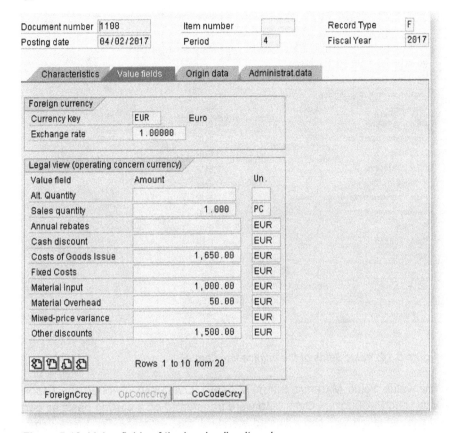

Figure 5.13: Value fields of the invoice line item I

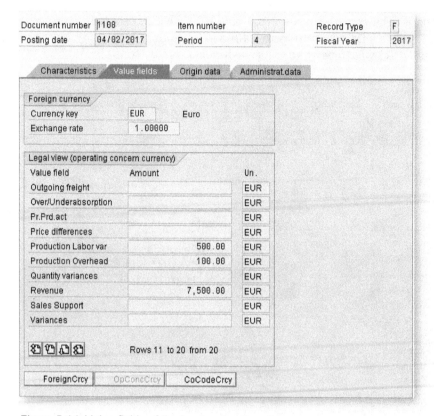

Figure 5.14: Value fields of the invoice line item II

The value fields MATERIAL INPUT, MATERIAL OVERHEAD, PRODUCTION LABOR VAR., and PRODUCTION OVERHEAD were transferred on a costing basis as part of the valuation with the adjusted standard cost estimate. For these items, nothing was posted to FI or to any other point in CO.

What changes has the invoice caused in our value flow (see the items highlighted)?

In CO-PA reporting, which you access via transaction KE30, the invoice has left the traces shown in Figure 5.16.

| | Finance (FI) | | Controlling | | | |
| | | Cost Center | Production Order | Profitability Object (CO-PA) | | |
P&L	Value	Value	Value	GP Structure	Actual Values	Cost-Based V.
Sales						
Revenues	-7500			Revenues	-7500	
Discounts	1500			Discounts	1500	
Inventory Changes				Net Sales	-6000	
Goods Received FERT	-1650		-1650			
Goods Received FERT	-360					
Goods Issued FERT	1650			CoS	1650	
Production Variance	360		-360	Production Variance	360	
Material Costs						
Consumption Raw Mat.	1000			Material Costs	1000	1000
Material Overhead		-50		Material Overhead	50	50
Manufacturing Costs						
Direct Labor		-800		Direct Labor	800	500
Manufacturing Overhead		-160		Manufact. Overhead	160	100
Wages Production	1500	1500				
Salary Prod. Mgt.	1000	1000		Gross Profit	-3990	
Wages Purchase	1000	1000				
Others						
Assessment CCA->CO-PA				Assessments		
EBIT	-1500	2490	0	EBIT	-3990	

Figure 5.15: FI/CO/CO-PA value flow (VII)

```
Gross Profit

Company Code Multiple values ➪
Sales Order Multiple values ➪
─Navigation──
Customer          ⊠Company Code  ▲ ▼ ⊕ ET11
Product           ⊠Sales Order   ▲ ▼ ⊕ 12298
Sales ord. item

⚲ 🄯 ✖
```

	Order Intake 04/17-04/17	Actual 04/17-04/17
Quantity	1.000	1.000
Revenues	7,500.00	7,500.00
Discounts	1,500.00	1,500.00
Total Revenue	6,000.00	6,000.00
Cost of Goods Issue	1,650.00	1,650.00
Production Order Var	0.00	0.00
Materials	1,000.00	1,000.00
Material Overheads	50.00	50.00
Production	500.00	500.00
Production Overhead	100.00	100.00
Calc. Prod. Costs	1,650.00	1,650.00
Variance Act vs.Calc	0.00	0.00
Gross Profit	4,350.00	4,350.00
Assessments	0.00	0.00
EBIT	4,350.00	4,350.00

Figure 5.16: CO-PA report with sales order and invoice

The invoice can be represented graphically as part of the logistics process, as shown in Figure 5.17.

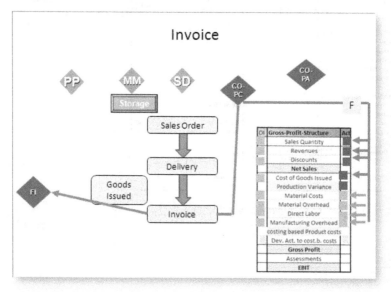

Figure 5.17: Invoice process

What does this graphic tell us exactly?

1. When the invoice is created the sale is posted to FI.

2. Furthermore, in CO-PA, line items are written for each invoice item. These line items contain the sales quantity, revenues, discounts, and costs of goods issued. These fields can be reconciled 1:1 with FI.

3. The other value fields describe costing-based values. In this case, the result of multiplying the sales quantity with the cost components of the adjusted standard cost estimate (from CO-PC) is represented in the corresponding value fields.

5.4   Reconciliation options with accounting

As we have learned so far in this chapter, when we save the invoice, important data is transferred to accounting. The invoice is therefore an important interface between logistics and accounting, and in particular, to CO-PA. Therefore, in this section, we will look at the options for reconciling the invoice with accounting. The following questions are particularly interesting here:

1. How can I reconcile my invoice sales between CO-PA, FI, and SD?

2. How can we reconcile the costs that were posted to FI at the time of the goods issue with the costs that were transferred to CO-PA when the invoice was created?

3. Has everything been transferred to accounting?

When reconciling the invoice with accounting, *periodization* is the first key-word to mention. Have my sales been posted in the same period—both in SD as well as in FI and CO-PA? Have the associated *costs of sales* been posted in the same period as the sales, in accordance with cost of sales accounting?

Another important question is whether all possible invoices have actually been issued! In SD, we use transaction VF04 to check whether the billing due list has been processed, at the latest at month-end closing. If this list is empty, you can usually assume that all required invoices have been issued. If the list does still contain invoices, these must first be triggered.

At this point, please note that we do not intend to explain all possible fine details in SD. Figure 5.18 shows a small screenshot from the SD application menu with the different application areas of this module.

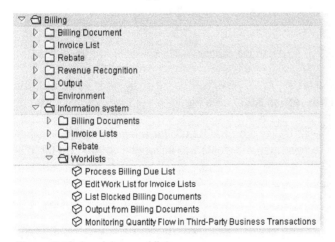

Figure 5.18: Invoicing worklists

5.4.1 Reconciling sales between FI and CO-PA

We will now look at reconciling sales. For our value flow described in this book, we are lucky because in Customizing, for the requirements classes we are using, we have defined that the sales order should not carry costs and revenues. What this means in reverse is that when we save the invoice, we can transfer the sales data directly to CO-PA.

Excursus: Reconciling sales

If the sales order carries costs and revenues, reconciling the sales is more complicated. The difficulty lies in the fact that the source of the sale in CO-PA is the sales order to be settled but in FI, the invoice is responsible for representing the sale. If you cannot establish a 1:1 relationship between the sales order and the invoice because you have two different sources, it will be difficult to reconcile the sales without a lot of effort (particularly if you find differences). If, for example, you have a sales order with multiple items, and these items were invoiced in different invoices and, to make things even more complicated, were invoiced to the customer in different periods, troubleshooting with an Excel sheet or reading information from the document flow table VBFA will be time-consuming. In contrast, if the invoice is the source of the sale for both FI and CO-PA, you can detect any possible variances more quickly because the source is the same.

Enough philosophizing, how can we reconcile the sales for our value flow?

Let's start with our analysis in CO-PA. You can display your sales with the report created with transaction KE30 (see Figure 5.19).

In FI, you can work with transaction FAGLL03, for example. In Section 5.3, we described that the revenues are posted to account **600000** and the discounts to account **600001**. We will now use these accounts for the selection for transaction FAGLL03 (Figure 5.20).

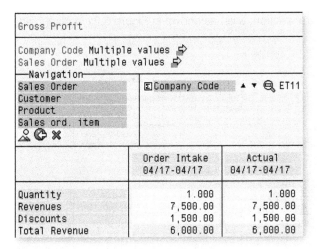

Figure 5.19: Invoice sales in CO-PA

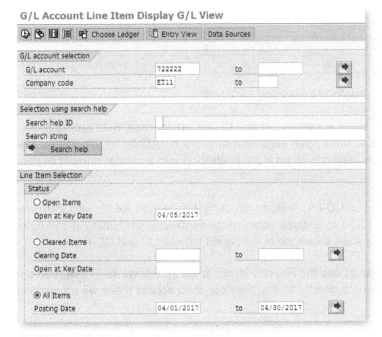

Figure 5.20: Selection screen for transaction FAGLL03

After we have run the transaction, a list as shown in Figure 5.21 is displayed.

G/L Account   600000   Umsatzerlöse
Company Code   ET11
Ledger   0L

	St	Assignment	DocumentNo	BusA	Typ	Doc..Date	PK	Amount in local cur.	LCurr
*	✓							7,500.00-	EUR
**	Account 600000							7,500.00-	EUR

G/L Account   600001   Erlösschmälerung
Company Code   ET11
Ledger   0L

	St	Assignment	DocumentNo	BusA	Typ	Doc..Date	PK	Amount in local cur.	LCurr
	✓		1400000005		RV	04/02/2017	40	1,500.00	EUR
*	✓							1,500.00	EUR
**	Account 600001							1,500.00	EUR

G/L Account   *   *
Company Code   *
Ledger   0L

	St	Assignment	DocumentNo	BusA	Typ	Doc..Date	PK	Amount in local cur.	LCurr
***								6,000.00-	EUR

Figure 5.21: Results of transaction FAGLL03

We can see that the sales for FI and CO-PA are identical (with only one document it would have been surprising to find a difference ...). Of course, this type of reconciliation is much more interesting with a greater number of documents.

Alternatively, in CO-PA, instead of using transaction KE30, you can use transaction KE24 to analyze your line items directly, particularly if you have discovered a sales difference in the period between FI and CO-PA.

Many companies use the *Report Painter* to set up reports for FI that read out the G/L accounts directly so that they can then access these via transaction GR55.

Of course, SD should also show the same sales as FI or CO-PA. To check this, you can use transaction VF05N, for example, to call up your sales in SD (see Figure 5.22)

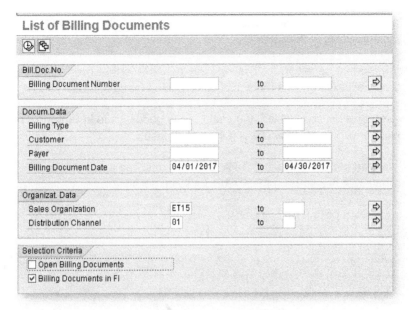

Figure 5.22: Selection screen for transaction VF05N

List of Billing Documents

BillT	Sold-To Pt	Payer	Billing Date	SOrg.	DChl	BlCat	Billing Doc.	DocCa	PsSt	Created	Net Value	Curr.
F2	K1	K1	04/02/2017	ET15	01	L	90036377	M	C	EIFLER	6,000.00	EUR

Figure 5.23: Results of transaction VF05N

In the results list (Figure 5.23) here, you see only the one invoice created for our example but if you have created a lot of invoices, you can use this transaction to reconcile your SD invoice sales in total.

5.4.2 Reconciling the costs of the goods issue between FI and CO-PA

As we have already learned, the time of the goods issue is decisive for the posting of the costs of the goods issue in FI. These costs are only recorded in CO-PA when the invoice is saved. Therefore, for clean periodization, it is important to ensure from an organizational perspective that the goods issue and the invoice are in the same period. This is the only way to ensure, in accordance with cost of sales accounting, that the sales are compared with the associated costs of the sales.

Another important condition for costing-based CO-PA is that condition type VPRS automatically contains the actual costs posted for the goods issue.

If both prerequisites are fulfilled, the costs of the goods issue in FI and CO-PA should agree. We will now check if this is the case.

Again, we start our analysis via CO-PA. Here we describe this process using transaction KE24 (transaction KE30 would also be possible).

Display Actual Line Items: Initial Screen

Selection Conditions				
Currency type	B0			
Record type	F	to		⇨
Period/year	004/2017	to	004/2017	⇨
Document number		to		⇨
Date created		to		⇨
Reference document number		to		⇨
Entered by		to		⇨
Sender cost center		to		⇨
Cost element		to		⇨
CO order		to		⇨
Sales order		to		⇨
Company code	ET11	to		⇨

Figure 5.24: Selecting invoice line items

Using record type **F**, we search for CO-PA line items that originate from invoicing (see Figure 5.24). In the list that appears, click CHANGE LAYOUT ⊞ to group the line items to meet your requirements. You could also use a previously defined line item layout. A standard layout is always used for the selection if you have not specified a layout in advance (see Figure 5.25).

We now check the costs of the goods issue in FI. You will remember that we performed the goods issue posting as follows (see Chapter 4, Figure 4.5): **893015** (Cost of Goods Sold) to **222222** (Finished Products) with the value **EUR 1650**

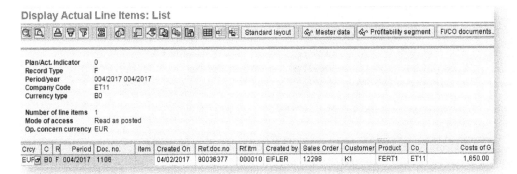

Figure 5.25: Invoice line items in CO-PA

Using expense account **893015**, we now call up transaction FAGLL03 again (see Figure 5.26).

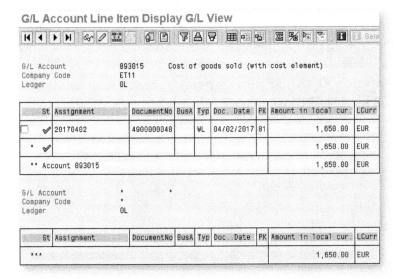

Figure 5.26: Costs of goods issue in FI

FI and CO-PA show the same costs of goods issue in the amount of **EUR 1650**.

137

5.4.3 Options for correcting sales or costs of sales in CO-PA

If you discover differences between FI and CO-PA in the sales or in the costs of the goods issue at the latest at the end of the period, how can you make adjustments in CO-PA so that both modules agree again? It depends ...

If there is an invoice error, the following generally applies:

Correction at the source

Correction documents are then created automatically in FI and CO-PA. To be more precise, in CO-PA, the previous line item is reversed and a new line item is created.

However, if the invoice is correct in FI and SD, but in CO-PA an incorrect value field is filled—perhaps due to an error in the CO-PA user exit—you can record this invoice in CO-PA again as described below.

Using transaction KE4ST you can simulate a new invoice transfer, which means that you can check whether a new invoice line item would bring about the desired result.

Using transaction KE4S you create a new invoice line item for the corresponding SD document (see Figure 5.27:).

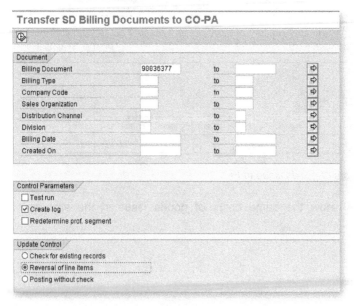

Figure 5.27: Selection screen for transaction KE4S

Figure 5.28 shows the result: two new CO-PA line items were created.

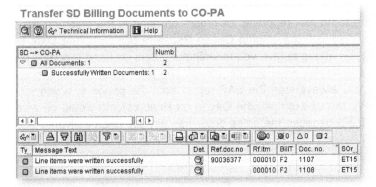

Figure 5.28: Results of transaction KE4S I

If you use the magnifying glass to look at the associated original document, in this case the invoice, and then click ACCOUNTING, in the expanded list (Figure 5.29) you will see that our invoice now has three CO-PA (Profitability Analysis) line items: the incorrect original line item, the reversal line item, and the correction line item.

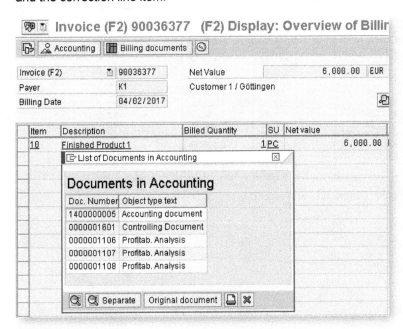

Figure 5.29: Results of transaction KE4S II

5.5 Excursus: Orders on hand reporting via CO-PA

Because there is no real reporting for orders on hand in the standard SAP system, you could add the column ORDER RECEIPTS MINUS ACTUAL DATA to the CO-PA report above to give you meaningful orders on hand reporting up to the sales order/sales order line item level. The prerequisite for this, however, is that you always start the SAP report from the period in which you started CO-PA. In our example, the ORDER ON HAND column would be zero (see Figure 5.30) because the sales order has already been delivered and invoiced:

```
Gross Profit

Company Code Multiple values ▷
Sales Order Multiple values ▷
──Navigation──
Customer            ▣Company Code   ▲ ▼ ⊕ ET11        E.T. Compar
Product             ▣Sales Order    ▲ ▼ ⊕ 12298
Sales ord. item

▲○✖
```

	Order Intake 04/17-04/17	Actual 04/17-04/17	Order on Hand 04/17-04/17
Quantity	1.000	1.000	0.000
Revenues	7,500.00	7,500.00	0.00
Discounts	1,500.00	1,500.00	0.00
Total Revenue	6,000.00	6,000.00	0.00
Cost of Goods Issue	1,650.00	1,650.00	0.00
Production Order Var	0.00	0.00	0.00
Materials	1,000.00	1,000.00	0.00
Material Overheads	50.00	50.00	0.00
Production	500.00	500.00	0.00
Production Overhead	100.00	100.00	0.00
Calc. Prod. Costs	1,650.00	1,650.00	0.00
Variance Act vs.Calc	0.00	0.00	0.00
Gross Profit	4,350.00	4,350.00	0.00
Assessments	0.00	0.00	0.00
EBIT	4,350.00	4,350.00	0.00

Figure 5.30: Orders on hand report

6 Assessment to CO-PA

As the last step in our value flow, we will now look at the cost center assessment to Profitability Analysis. This assessment is used to allocate the actual costs from cost centers to profitability segments to CO-PA.

6.1 The assessment process to Profitability Analysis

With this function, we can transfer the respective over/under absorption on our cost centers Production (KS1), Purchasing (KS3), and Production management (KS4) to CO-PA.

What does over/under absorption mean?

In our value flow, we have posted actual costs to three cost centers: wages to cost centers KS1 and KS3 and salaries to cost center KS4. During the production process, via the internal activity allocation of the personnel hours and the overhead costing, we have credited our three cost centers and debited our production order. The over/under absorption is the amount remaining on the three cost centers at the end of the day:

Over/under absorption = debits - credits

We can look at the over/under absorption on the cost centers using transaction KSB1 (Display Cost Center Line Items Actual Costs), for example (see Figure 6.1).

Cost Element	Cost element name	Cost Center		Val.in rep.cur.	Company Code
943111	Personnel Hours	KS1		800.00-	ET11
744444	Direct labor costs			1,500.00	ET11
		KS1		700.00	
744444	Direct labor costs	KS3		1,000.00	ET11
941111	Purchasing			50.00-	ET11
		KS3		950.00	
755555	Salaries	KS4		1,000.00	ET11
941222	Production Manager			160.00-	ET11
		KS4		840.00	
				2,490.00	

Figure 6.1: Over/under absorption on cost centers

Cost center **KS1**:

▶ Debit for direct labor costs in the amount of **EUR 1500**

▶ Credit for internal activity allocation (Personnel Hours) in the amount of **EUR 800**

▶ Over/under absorption in the amount of **EUR 700**

Cost center **KS3**:

▶ Debit for direct labor costs in the amount of **EUR 1000**

▶ Credit for material overhead (Purchasing) in the amount of **EUR 50**

▶ Over/under absorption in the amount of **EUR 950**

Cost center **KS4**:

▶ Debit for salaries in the amount of **EUR 1000**

▶ Credit for production overhead (Production Manager) in the amount of **EUR 160**

▶ Over/under absorption in the amount of **EUR 840**

Total: **EUR 2490**

Report for over/under absorption on cost centers

 The standard SAP report S_ALR_87013611 (Cost Centers: Actual/Plan/Variances) also shows, amongst other things, the over/under absorption on cost centers. This report is not a line item report. The debits and credits are shown as totals for each cost center and cost element.

Here you can select individual cost centers for a specific period or for a cost center area or an entire cost center group. The report/report interface in this report means that you can go to the line items (transaction KSB1) by simply double-clicking the respective line.

You transfer these over/under absorptions from the cost centers to CO-PA by executing assessment cycles.

An assessment cycle controls the sequence of an assessment and in the *segments*, contains all relevant control information on the senders (cost centers), receivers (profitability segments), sender and receiver rules, and allocation bases. The name and the start date form the unique key of the assessment cycle.

In the following we will create an assessment cycle with one segment for each cost center (KS1, KS3, and KS4) and then execute it and look at the result.

You can create an assessment cycle for CO-PA with transaction KEU1. In our example, we create the assessment cycle **ZUML** with start date **01/01/2017** (see Figure 6.2).

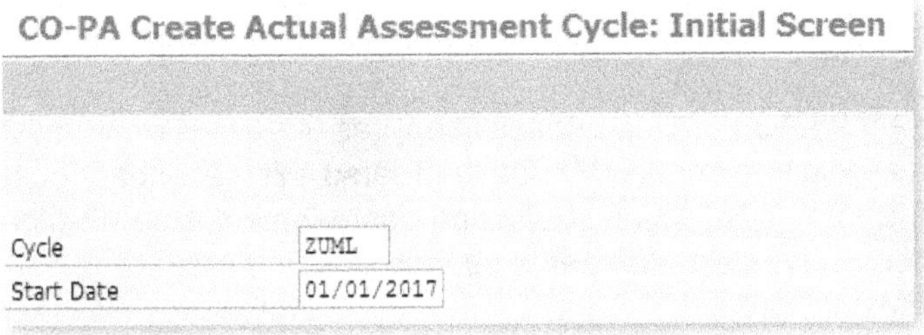

CO-PA Create Actual Assessment Cycle: Initial Screen

Cycle	ZUML
Start Date	01/01/2017

Figure 6.2: Creating a CO-PA assessment cycle

We press the `Enter` key to go to the header data for the assessment cycle (see Figure 6.3).

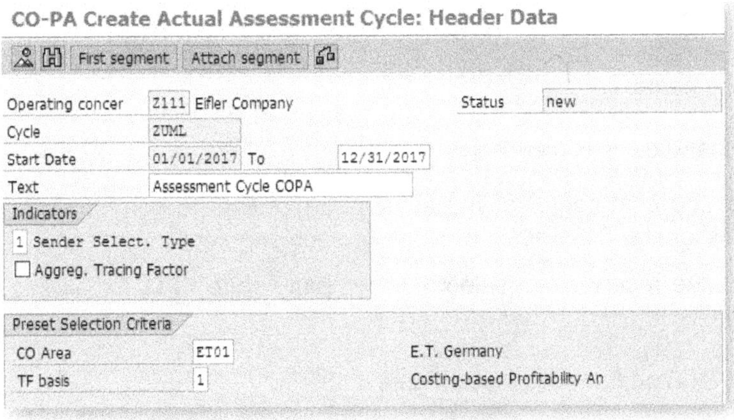

CO-PA Create Actual Assessment Cycle: Header Data

First segment   Attach segment

Operating concer	Z111 Eifler Company		Status	new
Cycle	ZUML			
Start Date	01/01/2017 To	12/31/2017		
Text	Assessment Cycle COPA			

Indicators
1 Sender Select. Type
☐ Aggreg. Tracing Factor

Preset Selection Criteria

CO Area	ET01	E.T. Germany
TF basis	1	Costing-based Profitability An

Figure 6.3: CO-PA assessment cycle: header data

In the header data, we enter the description **Assessment Cycle COPA**, select sender selection type **1** (Total Costs), our controlling area **ET01**, and **1** (Costing-Based Profitability Analysis) as the tracing factor basis.

We can then create our three segments by clicking ATTACH SEGMENT.

We have to enter the details explained below in the respective segments. You can track these settings via Figure 6.4 to Figure 6.6 as an example for the segment for cost center KS1:

SEGMENT NAME (see Figure 6.4):

▶ We name the three segments according to the cost center to be assessed (KS1, KS3, and KS4).

Tab SEGMENT HEADER:

▶ We select **942555** (CO-PA Assessment) as the assessment cost element for all segments. We have created this secondary cost element using transaction KA06 and cost element type **42** (Assessment). This cost element is used to post the respective credit to the cost centers.

▶ We enter value field **VV375** (Over/Under Absorption) as the receiver value field for all segments because this is where we want to transfer the over/under absorption of all cost centers to.

▶ We select **Posted Amounts** as the sender values for each segment.

▶ The receiver tracing factor should be **Fixed percentages** for all segments.

Tab SENDERS/RECEIVERS (see Figure 6.5):

▶ As the cost center of the sender, we select the corresponding cost center (KS1, KS3, or KS4) for each segment.

▶ As the receiver, we select our company code **ET11** for all segments.

Tab RECEIVER TRACING FACTOR (see Figure 6.6):

▶ As the receiver tracing factor (for our company code **ET11**), we enter the percentage ratio of **100%** in all segments.

With these settings, we ensure that when we run the assessment cycle, all over/under absorptions of cost centers KS1, KS3, and KS4 are transferred 100% to the value field VV375 with the characteristic **Company code ET11**. The credit posting to the respective cost center is posted with cost element **942555**.

CO-PA assessment cycle

 When defining an assessment cycle to CO-PA, you can configure a number of further or different settings. For example, instead of working with fixed percentages, you can work with fixed amounts; or instead of a fixed value field, you can select a PA transfer structure. Because the focus of our book is on the value flows to FI, CO, and CO-PA, at this point we will not go into any further detail of the additional options for defining an assessment cycle to CO-PA.

CO-PA Create Actual Assessment Cycle: Segment

◀ ▶ 🕮 👤 🖨 | Attach segment | 🔐

Operating concern	Z111	Eifler Company
Cycle	ZUML	Assessment Cycle COPA
Segment Name	KS1	KS1 ☐ Lock indicator

Segment Header	Senders/Receivers	Receiver Tracing Factor

Assessment CElem	942555	
Value Field All	VV375	Over/Underabsorption
Alloc.structure		
PA transfer struct.		

Sender values

Rule	Posted amounts ▼	
Share in %	100.00	

Receiver tracing factor

Rule	Fixed percentages ▼

Figure 6.4: Assessment cycle: segment header

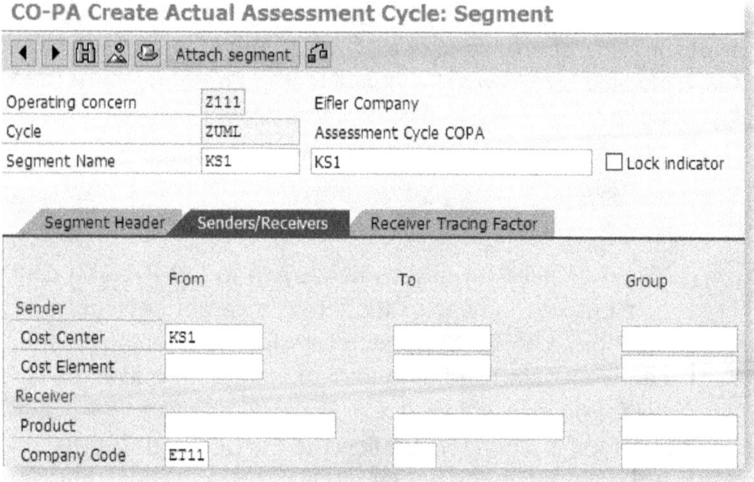

CO-PA Create Actual Assessment Cycle: Segment

◀ ▶ 🗊 ⚼ 🖻 | Attach segment | 🗗

Operating concern	Z111	Eifler Company	
Cycle	ZUML	Assessment Cycle COPA	
Segment Name	KS1	KS1	☐ Lock indicator

Segment Header	Senders/Receivers	Receiver Tracing Factor

	From	To	Group
Sender			
Cost Center	KS1		
Cost Element			
Receiver			
Product			
Company Code	ET11		

Figure 6.5: Assessment cycle: senders/receivers

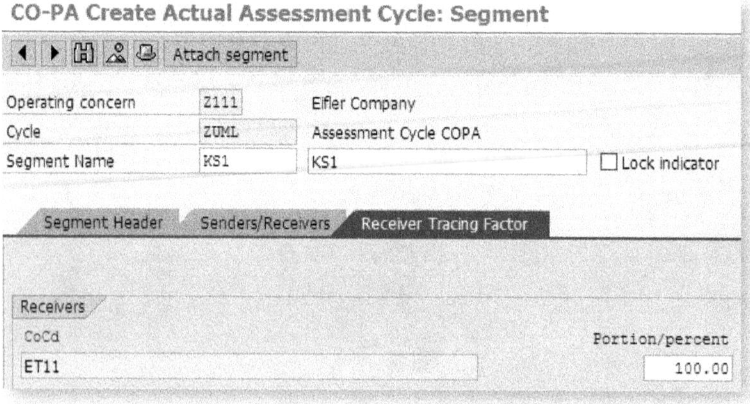

CO-PA Create Actual Assessment Cycle: Segment

◀ ▶ 🗊 ⚼ 🖻 | Attach segment

Operating concern	Z111	Eifler Company	
Cycle	ZUML	Assessment Cycle COPA	
Segment Name	KS1	KS1	☐ Lock indicator

Segment Header	Senders/Receivers	Receiver Tracing Factor

Receivers	
CoCd	Portion/percent
ET11	100.00

Figure 6.6: Assessment cycles: receiver tracing factor

Creating a CO-PA assessment cycle

Because users in the SAP system cannot create assessment cycles without special permissions, a transport request would be required each time, meaning that the cycles would have to be created in the development system and transferred to the live system via the normal transport route. It definitely makes sense to define creating/changing assessment cycles as "ongoing settings" so that these activities can be done directly in the live system. It is ultimately the end users who create these cycles and have to adjust them time and again.

Once we have created our assessment cycle, we can run it and thus transfer the over/under absorptions to CO-PA in accordance with the cycle definition. The transaction for this is KEU5 (see Figure 6.7).

Execute Actual Assessment: Initial Screen

⊕ ▣ Settings

Parameters

Period	1	To	1
Fiscal Year	2017		

Process with
- ☐ Background Processing
- ☑ Test Run
- ☑ Detail Lists   [List selection]

Cycle	Start Date	Text
ZUML	01/01/2017	Assessment Cycle COPA

Figure 6.7: Executing an assessment cycle

We select the relevant posting period, the fiscal year, and our assessment cycle **ZUML**. Before we post the assessment cycle, for safety's sake we can perform a test run.

List selection

Via LIST SELECTION you can display certain detail lists—for example of senders and receivers. By analyzing the results of the postings in the test run, you can define which senders and receivers are to be found and which values they are to be posted to with.

When we execute our assessment cycle as an update run, we get the result shown in Figure 6.8.

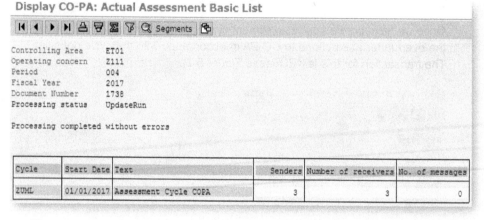

Display CO-PA: Actual Assessment Basic List

| ◄◄ ◄ ► ►◄ 🖨 🖥 Σ ▽ 🔍 Segments 🗗 |

Controlling Area   ET01
Operating concern   Z111
Period   004
Fiscal Year   2017
Document Number   1738
Processing status   UpdateRun

Processing completed without errors

Cycle	Start Date	Text	Senders	Number of receivers	No. of messages
ZUML	01/01/2017	Assessment Cycle COPA	3	3	0

Figure 6.8: CO-PA assessment cycle: update run

The following documents are created by the posting of the assessment cycle:

▶ Controlling document

▶ Profitability Analysis document

Remember: in this case, due to the real-time integration, no FI document is created; we explained in Section 3.2 that for our example, we selected the settings for real-time integration such that, for example, an FI document is only created if there is a change of functional area or profit center. There is no change of this type with the CO-PA assessment.

The first document is a Controlling document (see Figure 6.9). This document is created because the CO objects "cost centers" are credited with

148

assessment cost element **942555** (COPA Assessment) and a profitability segment is debited.

DocumentNo	Doc. Date	Document Header Text		RT RefDocNo	User Name	Rev RvT	
PRw OTy Object		CO object name	Cost Elem. Cost element name			Val/COArea Crcy	
⊞ 1738	04/05/2017 ZUML	20170101Assessment Cycle COP			THEIS		
1 REC Profit. analysis///		Profitability Analysis	942555			700.00	
2 REC Profit. analysis///		Profitability Analysis	942555			950.00	
3 REC Profit. analysis///		Profitability Analysis	942555			840.00	
4 CTR KS1		Production 1	942555			700.00-	
5 CTR KS3		Purchase	942555			950.00-	
6 CTR KS4		Production Managem.	942555			840.00-	

Figure 6.9: Controlling document

The second document is the Profitability Analysis document, whereby in actual fact, **three** Profitability Analysis documents are created because we have defined three segments in our assessment cycle. Figure 6.10 shows one of the Profitability Analysis documents created as an example. The assessment is transferred to CO-PA with record type **D**.

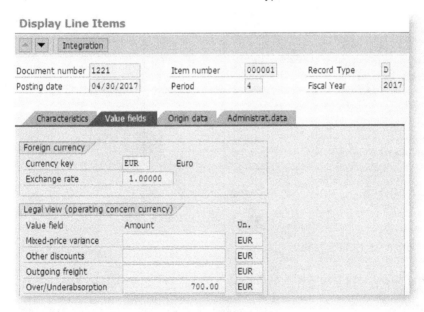

Figure 6.10: CO-PA document: assessment

If we look at transaction KSB1 (Cost Center Line Items Actual Costs) first, we can see that all cost centers have been credited via cost element **942555** (COPA Assessment) (see Figure 6.11).

Cost Element	Cost element name	Name of offsetting account	Cost Center	∝	Val.in rep.cur.
943111	Personnel Hours		KS1		800.00-
744444	Direct labor costs	Salaries and wages p			1,500.00
942555	COPA Assessment				700.00-
			KS1	🖫▪	0.00
744444	Direct labor costs	Salaries and wages p	KS3		1,000.00
941111	Purchasing				50.00-
942555	COPA Assessment				950.00-
			KS3	🖫▪	0.00
755555	Salaries	Salaries and wages p	KS4		1,000.00
941222	Production Manager				160.00-
942555	COPA Assessment				840.00-
			KS4	🖫▪	0.00
🖫				▪▪	0.00

Figure 6.11: Result of the CO-PA assessment: cost centers

Next, we take a look at our CO-PA report with transaction KE30. Here, the line ASSESSMENTS contains exactly our over/under absorption amount of **EUR 2490** (see Figure 6.12).

	Order Intake 04/17-04/17	Actual 04/17-04/17
Quantity	1.000	1.000
Revenues	7,500.00	7,500.00
Discounts	1,500.00	1,500.00
Total Revenue	6,000.00	6,000.00
Cost of Goods Issue	1,650.00	1,650.00
Production Order Var	0.00	360.00
Materials	1,000.00	1,000.00
Material Overheads	50.00	50.00
Production	500.00	500.00
Production Overhead	100.00	100.00
Calc. Prod. Costs	1,650.00	1,650.00
Variance Act vs.Calc	0.00	0.00
Gross Profit	4,350.00	3,990.00
Assessments	0.00	2,490.00
EBIT	4,350.00	1,500.00

Figure 6.12: CO-PA report

And finally, let's take a look at our value flow (see Figure 6.13).

We can see that with the assessment to CO-PA, the last step in our value flow has been completed. In addition to the production order, our cost centers have now also been completely credited.

Our value flow illustration shows that we have achieved matching EBIT in both Finance and Profitability Analysis: in both modules, our value flow is **EUR 1500**.

Finance (FI)		Controlling				
		Cost Center	Production Order	Profitability Object (CO-PA)		
P&L	Value	Value	Value	GP Structure	Actual Values	Cost-Based V.
Sales						
Revenues	-7500			Revenues	-7500	
Discounts	1500			Discounts	1500	
Inventory Changes				Net Sales	-6000	
Goods Received FERT	-1650		-1650			
Goods Received FERT	-360					
Goods Issued FERT	1650			CoS	1650	
Production Variance	360		-360	Production Variance	360	
Material Costs						
Consumption Raw Mat.	1000			1000 Material Costs		1000
Material Overhead		-50		50 Material Overhead		50
Manufacturing Costs						
Direct Labor		-800		800 Direct Labor		500
Manufacturing Overhead		-160		160 Manufact. Overhead		100
Wages Production	1500	1500				
Salary Prod. Mgt.	1000	1000		Gross Profit	-3990	
Wages Purchase	1000	1000				
Others						
Assessment CCA->CO-PA		-2490		Assessments	2490	
EBIT	-1500	0	0	EBIT	-1500	

Figure 6.13: FI/CO/COPA value flow (VIII)

6.2 Reconciliation options for the assessment cycle to CO-PA

Up until now we have discussed exclusively over/under absorptions on cost centers as part of the production process.

However, companies also have cost centers that are not credited via internal activity allocations or overhead costing in the production process—for example, the "Finance", "Marketing", or "Personnel" cost centers, to name just a few. These cost centers are debited with costs (salaries, travel costs, insurance, depreciation, etc.) and have a balance at the end of the month. There may also have been debits and credits via assessments between individual cost centers.

In order to reconcile the complete profit and loss statement with CO-PA at the end of the day, we can also transfer these cost centers to CO-PA via assessment cycles. The principle is exactly the same as the one described in this chapter.

In order to establish at period-end closing whether all cost centers have been completely credited and thus do not cause any differences between the P&L in FI and the gross profit report in CO-PA, we can use the report S_ALR_87013611 – Cost Centers: Actual/Plan/Variance (see Figure 6.14).

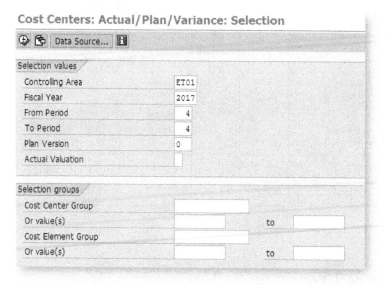

Figure 6.14: Selection screen for the cost center report

We can use various selection options for the report. For the check at month-end, for example, it would be useful to select the cost center group of the corresponding company code for the desired posting period. You can see the effects on the result of our value flow example in Figure 6.15.

The cost center report shows the primary postings that we originally execut-ed to the cost centers in the **Debit** total. Under **Credit**, we see our internal activity allocation (cost element **943111**) and the overheads (cost element **941111** and **941222**). On cost element **942555** we see the assessment posting of **EUR 2490** in CO-PA.

```
Cost centers: actual/plan/variance        Date:

Cost Center/Group          KS1,KS3,KS4
Person responsible:            *
Reporting period:              4  to    4  2017
```

Cost elements	Act.costs
744444 Direct labor costs	2,500.00
755555 Salaries	1,000.00
943111 Personnel Hours	
* Debit	3,500.00
941111 Purchasing	50.00-
941222 Production Manager	160.00-
942555 COPA Assessment	2,490.00-
943111 Personnel Hours	800.00-
* Credit	3,500.00-
** Over/underabsorption	

Figure 6.15: Cost center report

In comparison, we can display our original CO-PA report with transaction KE30 to check the result of the assessment in CO-PA (see Figure 6.16).

	Order Intake 04/17-04/17	Actual 04/17-04/17
Quantity	1.000	1.000
Revenues	7,500.00	7,500.00
Discounts	1,500.00	1,500.00
Total Revenue	6,000.00	6,000.00
Cost of Goods Issue	1,650.00	1,650.00
Production Order Var	0.00	360.00
Materials	1,000.00	1,000.00
Material Overheads	50.00	50.00
Production	500.00	500.00
Production Overhead	100.00	100.00
Calc. Prod. Costs	1,650.00	1,650.00
Variance Act vs.Calc	0.00	0.00
Gross Profit	4,350.00	3,990.00
Assessments	0.00	2,490.00
EBIT	4,350.00	1,500.00

Figure 6.16: Transaction KE30: CO-PA assessment

Furthermore, in CO-PA, we can also call up the CO-PA actual line item report (transaction KE24) again (see Figure 6.17).

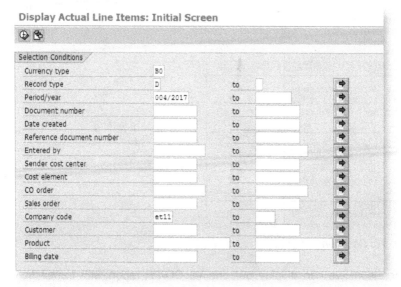

Display Actual Line Items: Initial Screen

Selection Conditions

Currency type	B0	
Record type	D	to
Period/year	004/2017	to
Document number		to
Date created		to
Reference document number		to
Entered by		to
Sender cost center		to
Cost element		to
CO order		to
Sales order		to
Company code	et11	to
Customer		to
Product		to
Billing date		to

Figure 6.17: Selection screen for transaction KE24

To run the report we select the currency type, the record type, the period, the fiscal year, and the company code. Figure 6.18 shows the result.

Crcy	C	R	Period	Doc. no.	Item	Created On	Ref.doc.no	Rf.itm	Created by	CoCd	Sender CCtr	Cost Element	Curr.	Σ	Over/Underabsorption
EUR	B0	D	004/2017	1221	000001	04/05/2017	1738		THEIS	ET11	KS1	942555	EUR		700.00
EUR	B0	D	004/2017	1221	000002	04/05/2017	1738		THEIS	ET11	KS3	942555	EUR		950.00
EUR	B0	D	004/2017	1221	000003	04/05/2017	1738		THEIS	ET11	KS4	942555	EUR		840.00
EUR													▪	**2,490.00**

Figure 6.18: Example report with transaction KE24

7 A further period-end closing activity: Work in process (WIP)

During our production process from the order receipt, through production and delivery of goods, up to the invoice and assessment to CO-PA, we have done a lot of work that is actually classic period-end closing work (overhead costing, calculation of production variances, and the assessment to CO-PA). There is also another task for period-end closing that we want to address in this chapter because it has an effect on the ability to reconcile FI, CO, and CO-PA: the *WIP calculation*.

7.1 The WIP calculation process

Let us call to mind our production order again and act as though goods issues, personnel hours, and the overheads had already been posted but our finished product has not been posted to the warehouse yet (see Figure 7.1).

Transaction	Origin	Cost Element	Origin (Text)	e	Total actual costs	Crcy
Goods Issues	ET11/RAW_MAT 1	733331	Raw Material 1		400.00	EUR
	ET11/RAW_MAT 2	733332	Raw Material 2		600.00	EUR
Goods Issues				■	1,000.00	EUR
Confirmations	KS1/999	943111	Production 1 / Personnel...		800.00	EUR
Confirmations				■	800.00	EUR
Overhead	KS3	941111	Purchase		50.00	EUR
	KS4	941222	Production Managem.		160.00	EUR
Overhead				■	210.00	EUR
Goods Receipt	ET11/FERT1	711111	Finished Product 1		0.00	EUR
Goods Receipt				■	0.00	EUR
				■ ■	2,010.00	EUR

Figure 7.1: Cost analysis for the production order

Until we have posted the goods receipt for our finished product, the production order still does not have the status **Completely delivered**. This status is the indicator which controls that at the end of the month, a WIP calculation is performed instead of the variance calculation. Figure 7.2 shows our current value flow image.

Finance (FI)		Controlling				
		Cost Center	Production Order	Profitability Object (CO-PA)		
P&L	Value	Value	Value	GP Structure	Actual Values	Cost-Based V.
Sales						
Revenues				Revenues		
Discounts				Discounts		
Inventory Changes				Net Sales	0	
Goods Received FERT						
Goods Received FERT						
Goods Issued FERT				CoS		
Production Variance				Production Variance		
Material Costs						
Consumption Raw Mat.	1000			1000 Material Costs		
Material Overhead		-50		50 Material Overhead		
Manufacturing Costs						
Direct Labor		-800		800 Direct Labor		
Manufacturing Overhead		-160		160 Manufact. Overhead		
Wages Production	1500	1500				
Salary Prod. Mgt.	1000	1000		Gross Profit	0	
Wages Purchase	1000	1000				
Others						
Assessment CCA->CO-PA		-2490		Assessments	2490	
EBIT	4500	0	2010	EBIT	2490	

Figure 7.2: FI/CO/CO-PA value flow (IX)

As you can see in the value flow image, the PRODUCTION ORDER column also contains our actual costs of **EUR 2010**. If we were now performing the month-end closing, we would transfer the over/under absorption of **EUR 2490** for our cost centers to CO-PA via assessment cycle.

If we compare the EBIT between FI and CO-PA, we see a difference: precisely the EUR 2010 of our production order.

In this case, the WIP calculation is missing for production orders that have not yet been completely delivered or technically closed.

In order to perform a WIP calculation, we have to meet various prerequisites in Customizing and we will now look at these more closely (see Figure 7.3).

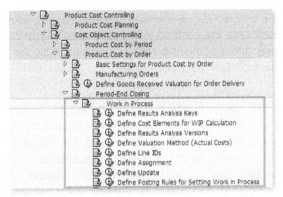

Figure 7.3: Prerequisites for a WIP calculation

▶ DEFINE RESULTS ANALYSIS KEYS

A WIP can only be calculated for a production order if a results analysis key is defined in the production order. We define the results analysis key using transaction OKG1. If the key is defined as a default value for each order type and plant, when the production order is created it is used automatically.

In our example, we have created results analysis key **FERT** (WIP calculation for production orders) and assigned it to our plant **ET11** and order type **PP01** as the default value. This key was then transferred to the header data when we created our production order (see Figure 7.4).

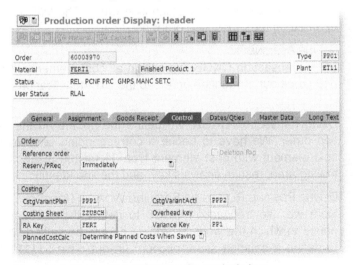

Figure 7.4: Production order: results analysis key

157

► DEFINE COST ELEMENTS FOR WIP CALCULATION
WIP cost elements are created with cost element type 31. This is used to save and update the results analysis data for the production orders on the respective order.

► DEFINE RESULTS ANALYSIS VERSIONS
You define the *results analysis version* in transaction OKG9. Results analysis data calculated via the WIP calculation is updated on the production order with reference to the results analysis version. In this results analysis version, you also define whether the WIP values are to be transferred to Finance. We have created results analysis version **0** (Version 0 Actual) with forwarding to Finance.

► DEFINE VALUATION METHOD (ACTUAL COSTS)
Using transaction OKGC we can define the *valuation method*. Here we have defined that the WIP should be calculated based on the actual costs (difference between debit and credit). Furthermore, the WIP should always be calculated when the status of the production order is **Released** or **Partially Released**; if the status is **Delivered** or **Technically Closed**, a previously calculated WIP should be replaced or there should be no WIP calculation.

► DEFINE LINE IDS
With the *line identification* we define how the total WIP amount is to be structured for each production order. The WIP amount is updated on the production order accordingly.

► DEFINE ASSIGNMENT
Using transaction OKGB, we assign all cost elements that debit and credit our production orders to the line identifications.

► DEFINE UPDATE
Using transaction OKGA, we define the *update* on the production order. We have to define a corresponding secondary WIP cost element with cost element type 31 for the respective controlling area, results analysis key, and the line identification.

► DEFINE POSTING RULES FOR SETTLING WORK IN PROCESS
Here we use transaction OKG8 to define the accounts in Finance to which the work in process should be settled. We have to define a balance sheet account (in our case **511111** (WIP))

and a P&L account (in our case **791111** (Inventory Change in Process)).

We will now execute and post the WIP calculation. We calculate the WIP with transaction KKAX (see Figure 7.5).

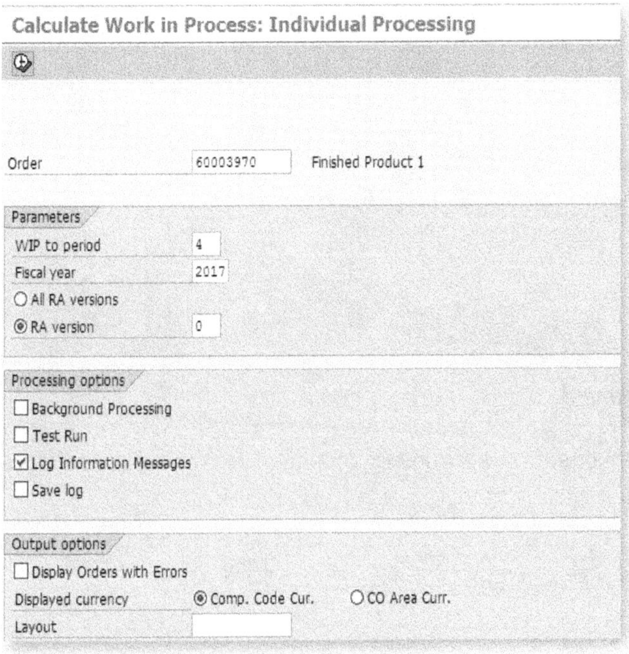

Figure 7.5: Performing the WIP calculation

We select our production order and specify the period, the fiscal year, and our results analysis version. We can see the results of the WIP calculation in Figure 7.6.

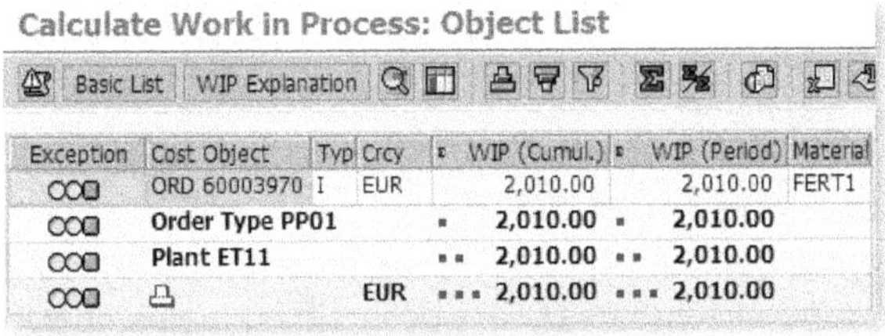
Calculate Work in Process: Object List

Basic List | WIP Explanation

Exception	Cost Object	Typ	Crcy		WIP (Cumul.)		WIP (Period)	Material
	ORD 60003970	I	EUR		2,010.00		2,010.00	FERT1
	Order Type PP01			▪	**2,010.00**	▪	**2,010.00**	
	Plant ET11			▪▪	**2,010.00**	▪▪	**2,010.00**	
			EUR	▪▪▪	**2,010.00**	▪▪▪	**2,010.00**	

Figure 7.6: Results of the WIP calculation

We post the work in process with transaction KO88 (Settlement) (see Figure 7.7).

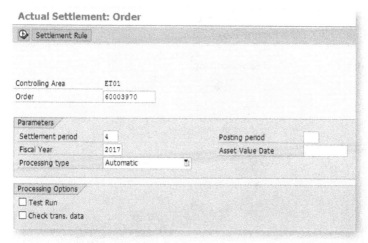

Figure 7.7: WIP settlement

After we run the settlement an accounting document is created (see Figure 7.8).

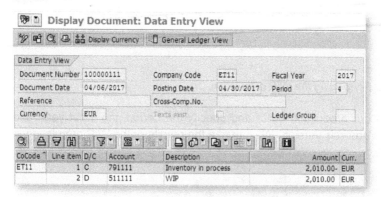

Figure 7.8: WIP: accounting document

The P&L account **791111** (Inventory in Process) was credited with **EUR 2010** and the offsetting debit entry was to balance sheet account **511111** (WIP). We can see the effect of this WIP posting in our value flow in Figure 7.9.

Finance (FI)		Cost Center	Production Order	Profitability Object (CO-PA)		
P&L	Value	Value	Value	GP Structure	Actual Values	Cost-Based V.
Sales						
Revenues				Revenues		
Discounts				Discounts		
Inventory Changes				Net Sales	0	
Goods Received FERT						
Goods Received FERT						
Inventory Change WIP	-2010		-2010			
Goods Issued FERT				CoS		
Production Variance				Production Variance		
Material Costs						
Consumption Raw Mat.	1000		1000	Material Costs		
Material Overhead		-50	50	Material Overhead		
Manufacturing Costs						
Direct Labor		-800	800	Direct Labor		
Manufacturing Overhead		-160	160	Manufact. Overhead		
Wages Production	1500	1500				
Salary Prod. Mgt.	1000	1000		Gross Profit	0	
Wages Purchase	1000	1000				
Others						
Assessment CCA->CO-PA		-2490		Assessments	2490	
EBIT	2490	0	0	EBIT	2490	

Figure 7.9: FI/CO/CO-PA value flow (X)

We can see that as a result of the WIP posting, we now have the same EBIT in FI and CO-PA again.

7.2 Reconciliation options for WIP

As already mentioned, when the WIP is calculated and updated in our example, no values are posted to CO-PA. Nevertheless, the WIP has to be calculated to maintain identical EBIT in FI and CO-PA.

What precisely is calculated depends on the status of the production order: if the production order has not yet been finally delivered or technically closed, WIP is always calculated; if one of these statuses has been achieved, variances are calculated.

We have already seen how to analyze and reconcile the variances in Section 3.4.

We can also clarify for the WIP calculation whether the correct WIP amount has been posted to FI. To do this, once again we use report FAGLL03 (G/L Account Line Item Display G/L View) in FI. Instead of the price difference account (as for the variances), we select the WIP account defined in Customizing. In our case, we have defined account **791111** (Inventory Change in Process) for the P&L posting line. Figure 7.10 shows the result.

G/L Account Line Item Display G/L View

G/L Account	791111	Inventory change in process
Company Code	ET11	
Ledger	0L	

St	Assignment	DocumentNo	BusA	Typ	Doc..Date	PK	Amount in local cur.	LCurr	Text
☐ ✔	60003970	100000111		SA	04/06/2017	50	2,010.00-	EUR	ORD 60003970
· ✔							2,010.00-	EUR	
** Account 791111							2,010.00-	EUR	

Figure 7.10: WIP: FAGLL03

For comparison purposes, let's look at the values of the production order with transaction KOB1. Figure 7.11 shows the result.

Cost Element	Cost element name	Σ	Val.in rep.cur.
733331	Consump. Raw Mat.1		400.00
733332	Consump. Raw Mat.2		600.00
941111	Purchasing		50.00
941222	Production Manager		160.00
943111	Personnel Hours		800.00
Order 60003970 Finished Product 1			**2,010.00**
			2,010.00

Figure 7.11: WIP: production order

We can see that it is precisely our WIP amount of **EUR 2010** that is left on the production order. We have now performed the following three month-end closing processes:

- ▶ WIP calculation
- ▶ Variance calculation
- ▶ Settlement

If we have been successful, the WIP amount posted in FI should agree with the total of all actual costs of the production orders in the corresponding period. If it does, we have done everything correctly.

8 The future of CO-PA under SAP S/4HANA

Guest contribution by Martin Munzel (Espresso Tutorials GmbH)

SAP currently recommends that with the new ERP system S/4HANA based on the in-memory database HANA, account-based CO-PA should "suddenly" become the method of choice. Have no fear: you will still have access to costing-based Profitability Analysis in the usual form under HANA and nobody will force you to replace it! Everything you have read so far in this book remains valid under HANA.

8.1 Who or what is HANA?

The term "HANA" was initially used by SAP as an acronym for "High-Performance **A**nalytic **A**ppliance". Today, *SAP HANA* is the proprietary name for SAP's in-memory database—a product that is offered either together with other SAP products, such as *SAP ERP* and *SAP BW*, or also separately (stand-alone).

This in-memory database features extremely fast analyses and aggregations of large volumes of data. But why does it provide such high performance? This can be attributed to a combination of multiple factors:

▶ In-memory means that all data is now stored in the main memory and not on the hard drive.

▶ All transaction data is organized according to columns in the database tables rather than lines.

▶ The HANA software uses the opportunities for parallel processing of data in modern hardware architectures to a high level.

The idea of outsourcing the data retention from the hard drive to the main memory is driven by the desire for significantly faster access times. And compared to the hard drive, for the main memory these are shorter by a factor of at least 100,000. Thanks to modern modular main memory components (blades) and constantly falling prices for the hardware, you can install in-memory databases with storage capacities of multiple terabytes, which is paying off for an increasing number of companies.

8.2   Changes with SAP S/4HANA Finance

Speed alone will not convince any SAP customer to switch to HANA. Instead, SAP is working feverishly at modifying their products ERP, BW, and others so that they have more to offer under HANA than just additional speed. The successor product to SAP ERP is called SAP S/4HANA and the application it contains for accounting is significantly different to ERP. In specific terms:

► FI and CO are merging

► Totals tables are no longer used

► A *universal journal* groups all information relevant for FI and CO in one single document

► Cost elements are no longer used; there are now only G/L accounts

The universal journal allows SAP to dispense with the existing separation of the individual accounting modules into submodules or ledgers and to ensure an extensive representation of and ability to analyze information in FI. Figure 8.1 shows the universal journal in graphic form. The documents are stored in the new table ACDOCA, which contains a lot of columns (currently more than 200) in order to map all possible information from the General Ledger (e.g., company code, G/L account, amount), Controlling, (controlling area, cost element [or rather, now the G/L account], cost center), Asset Accounting, and the Material Ledger.

In order to merge the diversity of information that comes from the different applications in accounting, SAP needs a characteristic that appears in all of these applications. With the removal of the cost elements, this characteristic is the G/L ACCOUNT. As you can see in Figure 8.1, the universal journal also contains a link to a PROFITABILITY SEGMENT (here referred to as a "Market Segment"). This allows direct access from FI documents to information from CO-PA. However, because the single common characteristic between the applications is the G/L account, the universal journal only works with *account-based* CO-PA.

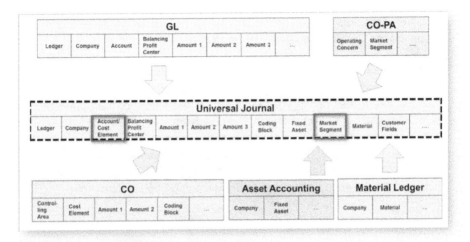

Figure 8.1: Universal journal

Account-based CO-PA has long since been in the shadow of the more powerful costing-based CO-PA. In account-based CO-PA you use cost elements instead of value fields. This has the advantage that it is easier to reconcile CO-PA data with FI because you do not have to derive the data from the value fields first. On the other hand, you can only represent content that is also posted in FI. In SAP ERP, therefore, in account-based CO-PA you cannot represent costing-based approaches such as the cost component split from product cost accounting, variance categories from PP, conditions from SD, overheads, or the order receipt from SD. To date, these limitations, along with performance deficits, have meant that most customers prefer to use costing-based CO-PA.

As already mentioned at the beginning, the introduction of SAP S/4HANA is causing some uncertainty amongst existing customers who have been using costing-based CO-PA for a long time. These customers are asking whether their module is thus becoming obsolete and whether they will be forced to switch. The functional gap that account-based CO-PA has compared to the costing-based version is causing further uncertainty. SAP has already made some adjustments here: on the one hand, they have upgraded account-based CO-PA in S/4HANA Finance by installing some of the functionality that has been missing so far. For example, you can now transfer the cost component split from project costing and actually post it with the goods issue. You can now also post the individual categories of the production variance to different G/L accounts. If this additional functionality is sufficient for your requirements, you should check whether it makes sense to switch to account-based CO-PA when you migrate to S/4HANA.

In contrast, if the costing-based approaches such as SD conditions, overheads, or order receipts are essential for your sales management, you will still be able to use costing-based CO-PA in the same form as previously—with all of the current advantages and disadvantages: you have full flexibility when mapping your sales management but have to do this outside the universal journal. Costing-based CO-PA will therefore remain a type of subledger, as it already is today. Just like before, you have to ensure that your profit can be transferred to FI, and this book will support you in doing that.

9 Closing words

Congratulations! You have managed to follow our representations of a value flow in an SAP system using a simple example right to the end. This means that you have worked your way through an entire book which has a new concept compared to other SAP books! We ourselves are often looking for books that describe complex topics in a clear and simple way so that everyone can understand them quickly. Our objective was to satisfy this need in our own book. You will find many SAP books that show all the options that the SAP software has to offer. That was not our intention. We have therefore presented, in as simple and hopefully understandable way as possible, how a value flow goes through the individual stages from a sales order, through production, up to the goods issue and invoice and where you can find these values in Finance (FI) and Controlling (CO).

In your company, you should use the CO-PA module as a tool for sales management—just as it was originally designed by SAP. It is not there solely for the purpose of reconciling your P&L again, even though in many companies there is a management requirement to be able to reconcile the P&L profit with the profit in a costing-based gross profit accounting. In this book we have shown how that can work, as the following final illustration shows (see Figure 9.1).

The EBIT in the P&L and the gross profit structure is identical at EUR 1500 in both cases (QED).

Now, you may well say: "Yes, that works with such a simple example but does it also work with the volume of data that usually arises in a company?" From our many years of experience, we can say: "Yes, it does also work with mass data!" The prerequisite for this, of course, is that you have customized the processes we have described correctly. You should also perform random checks on your value flow at regular intervals.

As long as you use the reconciliation options we have described (and the numerous reconciliation functions in the SAP system that we have not referred to) and—where necessary—the correction options described, your management will be happy when you provide further evidence that confirms the P&L profit.

| Finance (F) | | Controlling | | | | |
P&L	Value	Cost Center Value	Production Order Value	GP Structure	Actual Values	Cost-Based V.
Sales						
Revenues	-7500			Revenues	-7500	
Discounts	1500			Discounts	1500	
Inventory Changes				Net Sales	-6000	
Goods Received FERT	-1650		-1650			
Goods Received FERT	-360					
Goods Issued FERT	1650			CoS	1650	
Production Variance	360		-360	Production Variance	360	
Material Costs						
Consumption Raw Mat.	1000		1000	Material Costs		1000
Material Overhead		-50	50	Material Overhead		50
Manufacturing Costs						
Direct Labor		-800	800	Direct Labor		500
Manufacturing Overhead		-160	160	Manufact. Overhead		100
Wages Production	1500	1500				
Salary Prod. Mgt.	1000	1000		Gross Profit	-3990	
Wages Purchase	1000	1000				
Others						
Assessment CCA->CO-PA		-2490		Assessments	2490	
EBIT	-1500	0	0	EBIT	-1500	

Figure 9.1: FI/CO/CO-PA value flow (XI)

Over the long term, your management will be much happier about another aspect, however: with CO-PA, you have created a sales management tool with which you can enable the widest possible variety of business analyses and specifically, for all characteristics that you have provided in your operating concern.

By working through this book, you have also become familiar with the business progress of a logistical sales and production process using a simple example. Even better: you have learned how this process is mapped in an SAP system across the modules. Your management will also be happy about this because they know they have people who know the most important connections in an SAP system and can think outside the box. In today's global world, knowledge of (SAP) processes is a (competitive) advantage that should not be underestimated. Therefore, in future, do not allow yourself to be intimidated when someone says: "CO-PA is wrong!" As we have seen repeatedly in the process descriptions, CO-PA is the last module in the process. When errors occur, they are often application errors in the ongoing process; however, they only become visible or apparent in CO-PA.

We wish you every success in making your management happy—with your knowledge about values flows in the SAP system, in particular in Profitability Analysis, and with the supreme module of the SAP system itself!

Göttingen, May 2016

Christoph Theis Stefan Eifler

ESPRESSO TUTORIALS

You have finished the book.

Sign up for our newsletter!

Want to learn more about new e-books?

Get exclusive free downloads and SAP tips.

Sign up for our newsletter!

Please visit us at *newsletter.espresso-tutorials.com* to find out more.

A   The Authors

Christoph Theis studied business administration and now has more than ten years of experience in the SAP environment, with a focus on Financials and Controlling. Up until 2012 he was employed at Logwin AG. His main tasks included on one hand accompanying various international SAP rollouts with a focus on reporting, forms, Finance, and Controlling, and on the other hand, customizing the system, testing settings, training key users, and performing data migrations. For one year he managed the Cash Management department with nine employees and gathered extensive know-how as an employee in the Treasury and Controlling group at Logwin AG.

At the beginning of 2013, Christoph became an external SAP consultant and for one year, supported various medium-sized companies in SAP implementations and SAP optimization projects in the areas of FI and CO.

He now works as an accountant/in-house consultant for rollouts and integration projects with SAP FI & CO at Sartorius AG in Göttingen and supports international SAP rollouts in the areas of Financials and Controlling, for example in the USA, in Puerto Rico, France, Belgium and Tunisia.

Stefan Eifler has worked as an external and internal SAP consultant for more than 20 years, focusing on CO. He specializes in Profitability Analysis (CO-PA).

After completing his business studies degree at the Ruhr-Universität Bochum, Germany, Stefan began work as an external SAP consultant at COPA GmbH, a corporate consultancy specializing in the beverages industry, where he implemented the SAP module CO, including CO-PA, at many well-known companies. He then became an in-house SAP consultant at Berentzen-Gruppe AG. There, as the lead for Controlling projects, in addition to many SAP projects, such as the implementation of SAP R/3 when the Berentzen companies were merged into one company, Stefan was responsible for projects such as the implementation of international reporting (IFRS) for December 31, 2005. In additional roles such as Sales and Production Controller, Stefan was able to gather a lot of practical experience in Controlling. Due to his all-round business education and training, he also became the Risk Manager at Berentzen-Gruppe AG. Since February 2012, Stefan has been employed at the global company Sartorius AG in Göttingen, Germany, as an in-house consultant for SAP CO (Controlling). In addition to tasks as an IT delegate for Controlling, in third level support or as project manager for IT projects, such as a profit center reorganization, as a participant in a global

SAP rollout project, Stefan has been able to gather international experience in the USA, in Puerto Rico, France, Belgium, and Tunisia.

Stefan also holds presentations on CO-PA, for example as part of the FICO Forum info days. The idea of writing a book about value flows in Profitability Analysis together with his Sartorius colleague Christoph Theis came from these presentations.

For Stefan, this is his second book. His first book, "Quick Guide to SAP CO-PA (Profitability Analysis)" appeared in German in October 2012, was translated into English in 2013, and has since enjoyed successful sales worldwide. It is available in both print and Kindle versions, as well as in the online library of the publishing company Espresso Tutorials.

B Index

C Disclaimer

This publication contains references to the products of SAP SE.

SAP, R/3, SAP NetWeaver, Duet, PartnerEdge, ByDesign, SAP BusinessObjects Explorer, StreamWork, and other SAP products and services mentioned herein as well as their respective logos are trademarks or registered trademarks of SAP SE in Germany and other countries.

Business Objects and the Business Objects logo, BusinessObjects, Crystal Reports, Crystal Decisions, Web Intelligence, Xcelsius, and other Business Objects products and services mentioned herein as well as their respective logos are trademarks or registered trademarks of Business Objects Software Ltd. Business Objects is an SAP company.

Sybase and Adaptive Server, iAnywhere, Sybase 365, SQL Anywhere, and other Sybase products and services mentioned herein as well as their respective logos are trademarks or registered trademarks of Sybase, Inc. Sybase is an SAP company.

SAP SE is neither the author nor the publisher of this publication and is not responsible for its content. SAP Group shall not be liable for errors or omissions with respect to the materials. The only warranties for SAP Group products and services are those that are set forth in the express warranty statements accompanying such products and services, if any. Nothing herein should be construed as constituting an additional warranty.

More Espresso Tutorials Books

Martin Munzel:

New SAP® Controlling Planning Interface

► Introduction to Netweaver Business Client

► Flexible Planning Layouts

► Plan Data Upload from Excel

http://5011.espresso-tutorials.com

Stefan Eifler:

Quick Guide to SAP® CO-PA (Profitability Analysis)

► Basic organizational entities and master data

► Define the actual value flow

► Set up a planning environment

► Create your own reports

http://5018.espresso-tutorials.com

Paul Ovigele:

Reconciling SAP® CO-PA to the General Ledger

► Learn the Difference between Costing-based and Accounting-based CO-PA

► Walk through Various Value Flows into CO-PA

► Match the Cost-of-Sales Account with Corresponding Value Fields in CO-PA

http://5040.espresso-tutorials.com

Tanya Duncan:

Practical Guide to SAP® CO-PC (Product Cost Controlling)

► Cost Center Planning Process and Costing Run Execution
► Actual Cost Analysis & Reporting
► Controlling Master Data
► Month End Processes in Details

http://5064.espresso-tutorials.com

Ashish Sampat:

First Steps in SAP® Controlling (CO)

► Cost center and product cost planning and actual cost flow
► Best practices for cost absorption using Product Cost Controlling
► Month-end closing activities in SAP Controlling
► Examples and screenshots based on a case study approach

http://5069.espresso-tutorials.com

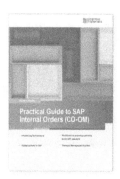

Marjorie Wright:

Practical Guide to SAP® Internal Orders (CO-OM)

► Concepts and daily postings to internal orders
► Master data configuration
► Streamlining period-end close activities
► Reporting options and summarization hierarchies in SAP CO

http://5139.espresso-tutorials.com

Ashish Sampat:

Expert Tips to Unleash the Full Potential of SAP® Controlling

▶ Optimize SAP ERP Controlling configuration, reconciliation, and reporting

▶ Transaction processiong tips to ensure accurate data capture

▶ Instructions for avoiding common month-end close pain points

▶ Reporting and reconciliation best practices

http://5140.espresso-tutorials.com

John Pringle:

Practical Guide to SAP® Profit Center Accounting

▶ Fundamentals of SAP Profit Center Accounting (PCA)

▶ Concepts, master data, actual data flow, and planning basics

▶ Differences between PCA in classic and new GL

▶ Reporting for Profit Center Accounting (PCA)

http://5144.espresso-tutorials.com/

Janet Salmon & Claus Wild:

First Steps in SAP® S/4HANA Finance

▶ Understand the basics of SAP S/4HANA Finance

▶ Explore the new architecture, configuration options, and SAP Fiori

▶ Examine SAP S/4HANA Finance migration steps

▶ Assess the impact on business processes

http://5149.espresso-tutorials.com

www.ingramcontent.com/pod-product-compliance
Lightning Source LLC
Chambersburg PA
CBHW052141070326
40690CB00047B/1345